Motivate
to win

3RD EDITION

Motivate to win

how to motivate yourself and others

RICHARD DENNY

KOGAN
PAGE

Motivators can be male or female. Throughout the book 'he' and 'she' are used liberally. If there is a preponderance of the masculine pronoun it is because the inadequacies of the English language do not provide a single personal pronoun suitable to refer to both sexes.

Publisher's note

Every possible effort has been made to ensure that the information contained in this book is accurate at the time of going to press, and the publishers and authors cannot accept responsibility for any errors or omissions, however caused. No responsibility for loss or damage occasioned to any person acting, or refraining from action, as a result of the material in this publication can be accepted by the editor, the publisher or the author.

First published in Great Britain and the United States in 1993 by Kogan Page Limited
Second edition published 2002
Third edition published 2006

120 Pentonville Road
London N1 9JN
United Kingdom
www.kogan-page.co.uk

ISBN 0 7494 4437 1

British Library Cataloguing-in-Publication Data

A CIP record for this book is available from the British Library.

Typeset by Jean Cussons Typesetting, Diss, Norfolk
Printed and bound in the United States by Thomson-Shore, Inc

For Lyster, Walter, Giles and Julius

The purpose of winning
The joys of sharing
The inspiration for success

A powerhouse of motivated sons

Contents

Acknowledgement

Thank you to Cathy Noon – always there when needed!

Introduction

The Institute of Manpower Studies has claimed that the word 'motivation' is among the six most-used words in company documents. It goes on to say that just because it is used, it doesn't mean to say that it is understood.

In a survey carried out by the Grassroots Group plc, which included 500 of the top 1,000 businesses in the UK, it was found that 95 per cent of those companies that responded felt their staff could be more motivated.

Martin van Mesdag, in a letter to *Marketing Week*, writes as follows:

> To motivate others is the most important of management tasks. It comprises the abilities to communicate, to set an example, to challenge, to encourage, to obtain feedback, to involve, to delegate, to develop and train, to inform, to brief and to provide a just reward.

This word motivation seems to cause extraordinary emotional reactions amongst so many people. Prior to writing this book, I discussed the concept with family, friends and colleagues and I seemed to get the universal reaction of 'I could do with it – whatever it is!' or 'I'll certainly look forward to reading that chapter'.

Motivation seems to provoke the response that everybody wants it but they are not quite sure what it is. We see in various job advertisements that the candidate must be self-motivated.

We also see the extraordinary results and achievements in the sporting world that are closely linked to the power of motivation.

Human beings, as we know, are natural goal seekers and it seems that all the amazing achievements in the world come from highly motivated individuals. We all live in a world of increasing complexity with incredible technology at our command. The developments of computer technology, microchips, the internet and the progress in electronic data processing and creativity fields are mind blowing.

Yet the real world in which we all work is, of course, a people's world. Parents produce children, those children go through their educational years and then move on to develop their own career. They in turn build relationships, get married and again children are produced. And so the cycle perpetuates itself.

Very few of us during our educational years had much, if any, instruction on ourselves, communication, people or motivation.

This book is about people; in business, in sports and hobbies, in relationships and their home environment.

Virtually everybody can motivate themselves and should be motivating somebody else.

How this Book can Help You

The point of writing this book was that it should be read, so it is written in a style that is easy to read. It should be a book that you can dip into and highlight certain phrases or paragraphs that may appeal to you. But its ultimate purpose is to take away the mystique surrounding that word 'motivation' and to set out easy and usable ideas that will help you to achieve whatever it is you want to achieve.

Success, as we all know, comes from people. Outstanding success is very rarely, if ever, achieved by the individual alone. It is achieved with the support, guidance, cooperation, advice, willingness and commitment of others, as well as the individual. How often do we see at the award ceremonies people receiving their award, then thanking others for their help?

A great deal of what this book contains could be classified as 'common sense' – that may be so and I make no apology for it whatsoever. Common sense is an admirable quality that those who have it tend to use and those who don't are not aware that it's lacking.

But due to the environment that we all live in, a world of rapid change, a world of increasing demands and increasing expectancy, perhaps the greatest requirement for all of us is that of self-improvement. How can we be better? How can we do better? And if we accept that the real world in which we live and work is a people's world, then it is essential to have a greater understanding of ourselves, what motivates us and how we can be more motivated.

Those of you who have the great responsibility of managing or leading others must know what is necessary to help people to achieve their own aspirations and how they can be motivated towards a common goal.

I have not set out to compile a series of motivational stories. The history of mankind is filled with the most amazing achievements of human endeavour: from outstanding performance in the world of sport to bravery in the theatre of war; from the financial success of the entrepreneur to triumph over life-threatening illness, or the personal sacrifices made by some to make life more bearable for the less fortunate.

Inner motivation is and always has been the power behind mankind's success and achievements. In building or maintaining your own motivation, search out those stories of success. It depends very little on your age, colour, creed or circumstances. YOU CAN, IF YOU THINK YOU CAN.

If you apply the principles discussed in this book, you will certainly be a more motivated person. If you have responsibility for others, you will certainly have a greater ability to achieve success through their success. **And your success is whatever you decide it to be.**

Motivation: a voluntary action in a given direction.

The Manager Is Dead – Long Live the Leader

If you understand what motivates people, you have at your command the most powerful tool for dealing with them.

In the Introduction, I said that motivation appears to be a general requirement. Everybody wants more motivation, but they're not quite sure what it is. The individual would say they would like to be more motivated. The manager or the leader would like to have a more motivated team or group, and the employer wishes to employ a motivated person. In fact, the employer's demands are even greater in that the person they need should be *self*-motivated.

Motivation and power are so closely linked that one can say there is power in a motivated person. You may recall that extraordinary story of the 5'4" mother weighing some nine stone who had a terrible car accident with her baby son on board. The car ended up on its side with the child trapped underneath. The mother was fortunately thrown clear and unhurt. When the rescue services arrived, they found the mother cradling her child in her arms, also unhurt. They were taken to hospital for a complete check-up, where it was discovered that the vertebrae in the mother's back had been crushed.

Apparently, what had happened was that she had lifted the car, removed the child with her feet and, in the process, damaged her back. There was no known way under normal circumstances that the mother could have lifted the vehicle. She did not have the physique, the strength or the muscle power. But she did have the **power of motivation.**

THE FOUNDATION OF ALL MOTIVATION IS HOPE.

Hope is therefore a criterion for people to be motivated. It is the cause for the effect – the fuel that drives the engine. Without hope, no person could ever be motivated.

Is management in its believed activity really redundant? I believe it should be. Historically, management was more about managing muscle than brain. It was the responsibility of the managers to think, to organize, to plan and then to convey clear instructions for their employees to carry out the tasks without deviation, hesitation or repetition. Nowadays, very little muscle is employed. What managers do have the responsibility for is the management of other people's brains, and probably one of their biggest frustrations is the often-voiced frustration, 'Why didn't you think?'

Therefore if you are hiring a person's brain, the old-fashioned management techniques really are redundant and have to be replaced by leadership, skills, behaviour and demonstration.

Motivation and Manipulation

Let us begin by distinguishing the difference from the management viewpoint between *motivation* and *manipulation*.

Manipulation, in my very simplistic view, seems to be getting somebody to do something because *you* want them to do it; whereas motivation is getting somebody to do something because *they* want to do it. And there is the difference.

As my great friend Frank Tijou said: 'It's the difference that makes the difference.'

For far too long in the recent history of business in the world, management has operated under a manipulative regime and nations have suffered from poor – and in many cases busy – management.

For a time, British managers actually stopped talking to their employees and communicated only through the unions. In all the years that I have been involved in business consultancy and training, I do not recall an instance where the real problem lay with the union. The problem lay in the boardroom with ineffectual, untrained directors cascading to management as the root cause of conflict. If the management style was to hide behind the closed office door, if the management style was not to communicate effectively, if the management style was to enforce, that's the way they did it.

I have already stated that the world in which we work is a people's world, yet still in many organizations, people are promoted into a management or leadership role because they were good at another job or task. Very rarely are people trained on how to manage others. Because they were good or effective in some other role, they are now expected by their peers to assume the title of manager and, by some God-given right, automatically know how to motivate, communicate with and manage others.

And so the cycle perpetuates itself because many of these managers follow the manipulative style of their predecessors.

Sure, manipulation does work. But it doesn't last and creates mistrust, leading to a 'them and us' situation.

A manipulative style of people management does not create the ideal where managers and their staff all pull together in the same direction to achieve their shared goals.

It is rather naive to encourage self-motivated people to attend an interview but expect the successful candidate to react kindly to manipulation when employed.

Motivation, as I have said, is getting somebody to do something because they want to do it. This also applies to you and me – if we really *want* to do something, we will be more motivated; and if we really *don't* want to do something, we will lack *self*-motivation. So throughout this book we shall be looking at and discussing methodology, principles and techniques, not only for building your own self-motivation, but also how to motivate other people with whom you come into contact. It is probably helpful to accept and understand the pain and pleasure principle. We, like the rest of the animal world, will do what we can to avoid pain. There is, of course, the natural instinct to avoid any likelihood of experiencing physical pain. Equally, we have a natural instinct to avoid any form of mental discomfort. Instances of this instinct include the reaction when faced with an unpleasant task such as the difficult phone call, the household chore, the meeting that could be confrontational, opening the bills, exercising in order to keep fit and giving up smoking.

On the other hand, we will go to great lengths in our quest to seek pleasure or perceived pleasure, which in some cases is short lived – eating too much, drinking too much. On the positive side, the drive for pleasure is, of course, crucial to achievement, as we will see when we look at goal achievement in more detail. The achievers of this world manage to get the balance of the pain and pleasure principle right.

We have to experience limited 'pain' from time to time, but whether you call this self-discipline or self-management is up to you. My good friend Steve Bennett, a successful entrepreneur and founder and builder of Jungle.com, encourages others to use his **BANJO** mnemonic technique.

> **B**ang
> **A**
> **N**asty
> **J**ob
> **O**ff

Many non-achievers procrastinate by putting off doing the important or nasty job, and in many cases do not expose themselves to any position where pain could be a possibility – unprepared to ever take a risk. When confronted with anything unpleasant, difficult, nasty or confrontational, Steve deals with it first using the 'banjo' technique. I recommend that, if you have two jobs to do, one unpleasant, one enjoyable, always do the nasty job first and then reward yourself with a nice task. I have always found this to be a successful approach. You and I both know that the person with little or no self-management will do the opposite.

In putting motivation into some perspective we must also distinguish the difference between **attitude motivation** and **incentive motivation**.

We all know of the 'carrot and stick' style of motivation. And as this is a view that many people still have of motivation, let us distinguish the difference between the two different kinds listed above.

Attitude Motivation

Attitude motivation is how people think and feel. It is their self-confidence, their belief in themselves, their attitude to life – be it positive or negative. It is how they feel about the future and how they react to the past. All of us from time to time have to make sure that we have the right attitude – but more about that later.

Incentive Motivation

Incentive motivation is where a person or a team reaps a reward from an activity. We can sum this up as: 'You do this and you get that'. Chapter 10 discusses incentive motivation in detail: the types of awards or prizes that drive people on, that get them to strive a little bit harder.

It is extremely important to understand the difference between the two kinds of motivation and to accept that both types are at their most effective when both are at work.

The Right Environment

As we go through the techniques of building motivation and putting the subject into its proper perspective, it is essential to understand that for an individual, a team or group of people, motivation can only be effective in the right environment.

For example, a manager may attempt to motivate a team of people by introducing a competition or incentive programme, which may well have been properly constructed, but if the environment in which that team is operating is not conducive to a harmonious relationship, there is backbiting, mistrust or an unhappy atmosphere, any incentive or attempted motivational approach will be ineffective.

So you must look at your environment – is it one in which you can be motivated? If you are a leader, is the environment right for your people to be motivated? Professor Hertzberg describes such considerations as 'hygiene factors'.

Take, for example, office facilities. Does the equipment work? Is the place too hot or too cold? Is it clean and tidy? How about lighting, fresh air, washroom facilities and, of course, workspace? Is it conducive to efficient work or are there other inhibiting factors to performance?

Are there realistic barriers that prevent you and your people achieving? The key word here is 'realistic' – I am not talking about excuses. Realistic barriers must be tackled, challenged and removed, and you must also accept that excuses are a mindset. They have to be changed, and in many cases this requires wilful determination and leadership.

To be an effective manager and motivator of others, one must have or develop leadership skills. This is common sense, but nevertheless worth repeating.

I personally love some of the great clichés, a good example of which is:

When the leaders are leading, the followers will follow

Of course, people copy their peers and one cannot divorce leadership styles from motivational results. 'Set a good example', leaders have been told since the beginning of time.

The Motivated Person

Let's now create an image of a motivated person. Our first impression is created by a person's appearance. A motivated person will surely have a smart outward appearance; their hair will look as though it has been taken care of, clothes will be pressed and freshly laundered, shoes clean. The outward appearance is therefore of somebody who cares about themself.

For a number of years, one of my companies ran a very successful telephone selling team. The standard was set and demanded that the telesales people always came to work smartly dressed, with good hairstyles and that the women wore make up. We found that the successful results were in direct correlation to the telesales team's motivation. When they felt good about themselves, so their output and sales successes rose.

There is a tendency to dress down in many companies. I do understand this more casual approach, but there is a balance to be struck. We all form opinions based on a person's appearance.

One should also notice the way people walk. I have one good friend who watches people arriving for an interview from his office window and he virtually makes up his mind as to whether he will hire them by judging the way they walk. He tells me that a person who walks with a purpose and with speed makes a better employee than a person who slouches and has a lazy walk. Do they amble along with their hands in their pockets or is there a spring in the step and arms swinging for propulsion?

Secondly, body language will convey a person's enthusiasm. A smiling face, sparking eyes and a positive facial expression can certainly convey an individual's motivation.

Students of body language claim that in this part of Europe, we are able to communicate with approximately 40,000 words and sounds, though on a day-to-day basis we habitually use just 4,000. On the other hand, body language signals conveyed from the face alone can number some 15,000.

We know that the majority of people can control what they say. So whenever body language is in conflict with the spoken word due to the sheer number of body language signals, the body language will almost certainly be conveying the correct information.

So somebody saying that they actually feel fine, but with a pained facial expression or stooped shoulders that clearly shows the opposite, can be studied, and their true feelings can be deduced.

Finally, how does a motivated person communicate? With enthusiasm. A motivated person talks about the future, what they are doing or planning to do. The past is used as experience to recognize and turn opportunities into success. The motivated person, therefore, has a zest for life and is a pleasure to be with.

And above everything else, a motivated person is what one could easily describe as a positive person. That is, showing the characteristics of an attitude that is:

- positive;
- motivated by a purpose;
- expecting to succeed.

This in turn generates energy. Motivated people seem to have an abundance of this. You have heard the expression: 'If you want something done, ask a busy person.'

Rewards = Results

Finally in this chapter, I would like to put motivation into some perspective by mentioning Michael le Boeuf's excellent book,

How To Motivate People, in which he describes the greatest management principle in the world, and that is:

> You get more of the behaviour you reward. You don't get what you hope for, ask for, wish for or beg for. You get what you reward.

The greatest management principle therefore suggests that the things that get rewarded get done. So you, as a manager or leader of others, must check and ask yourself – what do you recognize and reward? We will look in more detail at this in Chapter 8 under motivating the team and the group as well as motivating the person.

Fail to reward the right behaviour and you will most likely get the wrong results.

Pocket Reminders

- ▥ Hope is the foundation of all motivation
- ▥ Motivation or manipulation? – distinguish the difference
- ▥ Distinguish the difference – attitude motivation, incentive motivation
- ▥ Look for the characteristics of a motivated person

Wise Words

The common idea that success spoils people by making them vain, egotistical and self-complacent is erroneous. On the contrary, it makes them for the most part humble, tolerant and kind. Failure makes people cruel and bitter.

Somerset Maugham

2

The Laws of Motivation

For those of you reading this book who have that great responsibility of managing, leading and motivating others, let me ask you these two questions:

What sort of manager would you like to be managed by?

Get a clear picture in your mind, and then compile a list of all the manager's characteristics below. Do not think about your current manager; instead think about the most perfect manager/leader – what would be their characteristics? May I suggest a few? He or she would be positive, enthusiastic and a good communicator with a clear purpose, plans and goals. He or she would make my days at work enjoyable and fulfilling. If I did something wrong, this person wouldn't shout or scream at me, but ask me how I could do it better next time and what I had learnt from my mistake. If I did something well, I would be given lots of praise.

_____

_____

_____

_____

The second question, and the toughest, is:

Are you that sort of person?

You see, you don't have to do to others what may have been done to you. You alone are responsible for your own actions and you alone are responsible for the happiness and achievement of the people in your care and responsibility. Your actions with your employees at work will have a direct bearing on their overall happiness in their private life. We all know that people who are happy at work are more likely to be happy at home, but if they are unhappy at work, it is almost impossible to be happy at home.

These are two really pertinent and soul-searching questions, which every manager should ask him or herself regularly, as the answers must build a foundation for the principles that will be conducive to a healthy management style. I try to ask myself these questions every day when I have the great responsibility of managing and leading others.

In this chapter we will look at the laws of motivation. One could argue that they are *principles* rather than laws, but I prefer to use the word 'laws' because it implies that if you break them, you will receive a penalty.

LAW 1

We Have to be Motivated to Motivate

It is impossible to motivate another person if you yourself are not motivated.

What sort of manager do you want to be managed by? The manager who arrives at work before anybody else, who is enthusiastic, positive, always has a bit of good news to pass on, is loyal and leads by example? A manager who has a purpose – in other words, a MOTIVATED MANAGER?

I have met so many managers who demand and expect their

employees to be more motivated, yet looking at these managers, it is absolutely apparent why they are not getting what they hope for.

I chaired a conference for some 200 senior managers of a major UK public company. It became apparent that this was their second conference at attempting to launch a new management style and strategy. However, the new system was not fully understood and had not been enthusiastically embraced by the senior executives. It came to light that one of the root causes for the lack of enthusiasm and motivation to change lay on the shoulders of one person. The key manager responsible for the roll-out of the programme had been made redundant shortly before the first conference and was then invited back for a six-month contract just to communicate and implement the strategy. What an odd management decision!

If you want to motivate another person, you have to be motivated yourself.

LAW 2
Motivation Requires a Goal

It is impossible for any individual, or for that matter, any team or group of people, to be motivated without a clear and specific goal. This point is so obvious it may be just common sense to some people, and so may be irritating for me to emphasize its importance here. However, in the business world, it is common sense that is simply not commonly recognized.

In the world of sport, the opposite is the reality. It is obvious that a team cannot be motivated by the captain, manager or coach without a competition or an objective to strive for. Can you imagine a team sport, football for example, where there is no league or competition that they can be part of? It would be impossible for the coach to motivate that team in order to get the best out of the players. The coach almost certainly wouldn't even be able to get them to attend practice or coaching sessions. One of the great challenges of modern-day football management is to motivate the teams that are filled with incredibly highly paid players. As the players are paid so much money, it is almost impossible to motivate them with reward. Therefore the managers often create conflict between themselves, thereby creating enemies.

If I were to ask any of your people what is the goal for the day, would they be able to tell me? Could they tell me the goal for the week or the month? They might be able to tell me the goal for the year, but it is important to remember that long-term goals have no immediate effect.

Motivation, as I have already said, is about striving towards the future and without a goal, there is no purpose.

In Chapter 6 on how to motivate yourself, I will be looking at and discussing the principles and the stages of goal setting and how to get whatever it is you want. It is sad that so few people do have goals and even more devastating that many have no hope. In fact, some people wake up in the morning and their first reaction is one of surprise – they have survived the night! They have no purpose, no goals and nothing that they are looking forward to achieving or doing.

We all know how apathy can creep in when there is no hope. All of us must have hope. We must be looking forward to something and so goals and objectives must be set.

LAW 3

Motivation, Once Established, Never Lasts

This law stems from a common management misjudgement. I attend many conferences every year and one of the main objectives of company conferences is to get everybody together, impart information on past performance, tell them the news and set out the goals and plans for the future. The overall objective is to send the participants and delegates back home with their batteries recharged and highly motivated. And most conferences do achieve that objective.

But that motivation and warm feeling does not last. It is a bit like blowing up a balloon – if you don't tie a knot in the neck the air will come back out again. Motivation should and must be an ongoing process. It is not a once-a-year booster.

Some organizations have a yearly appraisal where each member of staff meets for private discussion with their superior and their performance is appraised. This, of course, can be a motivational exercise or a demotivational one. But the purpose of appraisal, if it is conducted correctly, is motivational – where one discusses strengths and weaknesses and draws up plans of action and self-improvement for the future.

The most effective appraisal is of course what is known as the 360-degree appraisal. This is when the manager is also appraised by each staff member in his or her direct line of reporting. I equally believe that people who have the task of appraising must also be trained for it to be effective, worthwhile and motivational. However, important as the yearly or half-yearly appraisal may be, a really good leader appraises daily, possibly even hourly – not formally, of course, but by watching, listening and discovering where help or guidance may be needed.

However, in some organizations, this is the only time a person's performance is discussed with a superior – just once a year. Therefore, accepting the appraisals can be motivational, apart from the essential requirement of correcting unproductive performance or behaviour, it makes sense to have a more regular, perhaps quarterly, schedule of mini-appraisals as well.

But this is only one example of ongoing motivation. We will be looking at numerous ideas on how to motivate people as we go through this book. However, be aware that just because an individual might be motivated today, it doesn't mean they will be motivated tomorrow.

A person can be motivated at their workplace and be demotivated in their home environment and vice versa. This alone is a good enough reason why every individual should understand the power of motivation, understand themselves, how they feel and why they react; what causes them to be happy or unhappy and what inspires them to do just that little bit more.

We must all understand what really demotivates us and then as frequently as possible take steps to prevent it happening.

Ask yourself, and be totally honest and realistic – what really demotivates you (both in your business life and in your private life)? A greater understanding of yourself will also be effective in managing and leading others. Do you feel demotivated by pressure at work or monetary worries, or is it just silly little things that really irritate you?

Leaders and managers must create events that will be *motivational*. It is just not good enough to have only one event a year that gives people a lift or a recharge. It should be an ongoing, planned process.

LAW 4
Motivation Requires Recognition

This is such a powerful law. Continue to break it and you will never have people around you who are truly motivated. This is so much more important than money – people must feel valued and respected. Do you treat your employees as you would your best customers? People don't leave companies; they leave people.

Recognition comes in so many different forms: from the peerage to the 'thank you' letter; from the way you introduce somebody to the admiring of a flower arrangement; from the Oscar to the new job title; from the certificate to the invitation to be on a committee; from a photo in the newspaper to an appearance on television.

People will strive harder for recognition than for almost any other single thing in life. Recognition can be a compliment. If you are a parent, you have no doubt experienced your child returning home from school with some work. It may be a picture he or she has painted, and you as a parent admire that picture, show it to other members of the family and pin it up on the wall. The result will be, as I am sure you have noticed, not only a motivated child but also more pictures.

Genuine compliments are a form of recognition and it takes a thoughtful person to give another a compliment. Small-minded people are unable ever to recognize the achievements of others.

In businesses, companies give recognition at conferences, where they thank members of staff for performance, achievement, loyalty, etc. It is a golden rule that, when giving recognition, nobody should be forgotten.

At one particular conference I attended, the chairman was awarding bottles of champagne to star performers and these bottles had been earnt by sales volume achieved. As he finished handing out the last bottle, he asked the audience whether he had left anybody out. One poor individual raised his hand in the air. A dumbfounded expression appeared on the chairman's face and he was overheard to say to the assistant on the platform: 'Who the bloody hell is that?' Fortunately, the assistant knew the salesperson's name. They both peered into a bundle of record forms and in due course the chairman announced that, yes, the individual was right. They had made a mistake but, luckily, they had a spare bottle and the poor fellow came to get his reward. An otherwise successful recognition event had been devalued.

LAW 5

Participation Motivates

This law has been proven in almost every environment where people are truly effective. It is vital to get people involved and seek their opinions. Over the years, working with so many different organizations, I have repeatedly found that employees within an organization have brilliant ideas on improvement, cost-saving, efficiency and time usage but there is no mechanism for them to share or communicate those ideas with their managers or directors. If only more directors would listen to their staff, their companies would be so much more effective.

Julian Richer, the founder of the incredibly successful hi-fi retailer Richer Sounds (which has been in the *Guinness Book of Records* for over eight years for selling more hi-fi per square foot of retail space than any other retailer in the world), says that when he started his company 100 per cent of the ideas came from him. Nowadays, 90 per cent of how the company is run, including its systems and procedures etc, comes from his people; only 10 per cent comes from him. All members of staff had to give 20 ideas per year for improvement, in order to retain their jobs. For each idea they were rewarded a minimum of £5, and this rose according to the value of the idea. He has given away £15,000–£20,000 to Richer Sounds employees for the contribution and the usage of their ideas. Every idea that was put up would have a response within three days from a senior manager or a director, indicating either why the idea could not be implemented or whether action would be taken. The consequence has been a stream of innovation, but, more importantly, Richer Sounds has an incredibly high staff retention, which is unusual for high street retailers. There is normally a list of people waiting for a vacancy.

I have attended so many conferences where delegates are broken into syndicate sessions, the flip chart is produced and new ideas and improvements are written up. At the end of the conference those flip charts end up in some dustbin, no action is taken and no feedback is given. This is such a big opportunity for every manager to turn his or her style into one of leadership.

LAW 6
Seeing Ourselves Progressing Motivates Us

This is another law that you must understand fully. When we see ourselves progressing, moving forward and achieving, we will always be more motivated. When we see ourselves going backwards, we will be demotivated.

This, of course, like so many of these laws, is common sense. But as we all know, common sense is not very common! There was a period of time in the UK when, after several years of property values increasing, they then declined, and in some parts of Britain a 50 per cent drop was common. Householders with mortgages suddenly experienced negative equity in their most valuable possession. While house prices were on the rise, the nation was buoyant, and it was often described as the 'feel-good factor'. With the drop in house prices came negative equity and demotivation. Most of us in the period between Christmas and the New Year review the past year. If it has generally been good and we have reduced the mortgage, saved a little, perhaps got promoted or improved our lifestyle, we will go into the New Year with greater enthusiasm. If, on the other hand, the past year hasn't been so good, it is then very understandable that we might approach the future with a little bit of uncertainty and less motivation. It requires a greater concentration of the mind to learn from the past (which we cannot change) and turn it to our advantage by learning from mistakes made and experiences understood. So, in business, leaders will find some area of activity where there is improvement and will highlight it and share it with their people, focusing on the progression rather than dwelling continually on the negative results.

I have met many people who find tremendous peace of mind after bankruptcy. The devastating period of desperation and worry is removed once the bankruptcy takes place. From then on, they can only go back up again.

It's the fear of wondering what else can go wrong that causes the demotivated feeling.

It is a human characteristic that, when we see ourselves achieving progress, we are definitely more motivated. Whether in our private or business life, our hobbies, sports or interests, when we see ourselves moving forward, we just want to go further.

We experience the feelgood factor. Leaders will ensure that their people are informed of the slightest progress. In tough times, the leader will re-emphasize some point or some activity that the team is making progress with.

This law has to be used, worked on, managed and planned in order to maintain a high level of motivation.

LAW 7

Challenge Only Motivates If You Can Win

Later on in the book we will be looking at incentives, competitions and challenges to inspire people to greater performance. But a challenge will only motivate a person if they think they have a chance of success.

I have seen too many contests and competitions organized by sales managers with the object of inspiring people to greater sales results. They have not understood this law and then wondered why only one or two people were motivated by the contest to raise their performance, grasp the challenge and reap the reward.

Managing directors, sales directors and managers, please don't set targets too high – be realistic. Frustratingly, some think that big targets are motivational because they are a challenge. If the consensus is that the target is impossible, demotivation will be the result.

Contests, competitions and challenges are extremely effective and most certainly do inspire people to greater activity. But those who should be participating must believe that they have a chance to win.

I have seen an instance where a company provided a two-week holiday for two in the Bahamas as a prize. It was open to all members of a forty-strong sales force. The prize was to be awarded to the person who got the most sales in a three-month period. Three people out of the sales team of forty set out on the challenge. These three had the biggest area by territory, had the biggest volume of customers and enquiries all ready to handle. They had also consistently been in the top three for the previous two years. The remainder of the sales force were actually demotivated by this challenge, as they knew they had little or no chance of success. The difference between them and the first three was so vast that it was near enough impossible to make up the ground.

Challenge does motivate. People will rise to the occasion. Challenge them to get something worthwhile done and nine times out of ten they will do it. More and more managers are finding that work in itself can be a motivator. Not just work as drudgery, but other aspects of work such as responsibility, challenge and a feeling of doing something worthwhile.

One can make a person's work more challenging by giving them the biggest job they can handle – and with this responsibility must, of course, come the credit of achievement.

LAW 8
Everybody Has a Motivational Fuse

This law says that everybody can be motivated. A person may have the fuse but we don't know at what point it will ignite. Sometimes it is just not cost-effective to continue trying to spark a person into activity or greater performance.

Each one of us has a fuse, and an effective motivational manager will try many ways to spark somebody into a more motivated mode of behaviour. When this is attempted and fails, the manager in many cases blames himself. For any manager one of the most unpleasant duties is to fire an employee. But sometimes this can be the best course of action because, as we have already said, it may be the environment that is producing bad performance. On the other hand, it could be the individual who is determinedly unwilling to change, the individual who perpetually points the finger and says: 'It's not my fault, it's everybody else's. It's the company, the product, the paperwork. It's the manager. In fact, my job is a lousy job.'

It must be remembered that the job does not care about people. It is a person's attitude to a job that makes the difference. A person can quite emphatically state and believe that theirs is the worst job humanity has ever created. Yet another taking on that same job with a different attitude will say and believe it is a great job and will consider themself fortunate to have it.

So in handling this law, as a motivator, you must understand that everybody does have a fuse and they can be sparked into life. Equally, you must accept that sometimes the effort and time involved just might not be cost-effective.

LAW 9

Group Belonging Motivates

This law emphasizes the importance of people having a feeling of belonging. The smaller the unit to which they belong, the greater their loyalty, motivation and effort.

When you were at school, there may have been a school team and house teams. I suggest that when the house teams were playing each other, greater excitement, emotion, loyalty and motivation was apparent than when the school team was playing.

Let's extend this analogy. What causes more emotion amongst supporters and in turn raises the ticket prices on the black market – is it the league cup final or the national team playing another country? The supporters of local teams show who they belong to by wearing the scarves, the hats and the badges of their team – they want to belong.

Everybody, of course, is an 'employee' by being part of a company or organization, but a good motivational manager will also make their people part of a team.

In some cases, it may be a name that is created; for example, the leader of the team's surname is used as the team name. In other organizations, teams are formed within departments: the production department, the marketing department, the sales department and so on. And where this feeling of group belonging is created, the good motivational manager will create extra-curricular activities that draw their people together. These might include a summer barbecue, a trip to the theatre or regular team meetings and briefings. T-shirts, pens and diaries can also create a feeling of belonging to a team. **But do accept that group belonging motivates people.**

LAW 10
Inspired Leadership Is Motivational

This is again the difference between a manager and a leader. Leaders will inspire people by their actions. Leaders will take a risk, which will, of course, be calculated. Leaders will be continually looking for new challenges and new opportunities. People are much more motivated to be loyal and supportive with inspired leadership. In nearly every business there are occasions when the manager must defend his or her people from criticism or attack by others. It is on those occasions that leadership replaces management – the leader will defend his or her own people and will take full responsibility for the criticism.

Pocket Reminders

- We have to be motivated to motivate
- Motivation requires a goal
- Motivation, once established, never lasts
- Motivation requires recognition
- Participation motivates
- Seeing ourselves progress motivates us
- Challenge only motivates if you can win
- Everybody has a motivational fuse
- Belonging to a group motivates
- Inspired leadership is motivational

Wise Words

A man persuaded against his will retains the same opinion still.

Howard Lago

3

Recognize the Demotivators

Just as important as knowing the rules of motivation is to know and be able to recognize the demotivators. The foundation of all motivation, as discussed earlier, is hope. Without hope, an individual is going to be without motivation.

Mankind is a goal-striving animal. The history of mankind goes from one goal achievement to another and it is this looking forward to the future that immeasurably helps towards creating a motivated mind.

A person who lacks motivation or who has been demotivated by others or by circumstances will show through their body language, their appearance and facial expressions how they are feeling. It is essential, therefore, to recognize the outward signs of the unmotivated person.

This, of course, is common sense, but due to the pressure and the pace of life that most people lead, all too often they are not conscious of other people's feelings. This is why it is so important for a motivated manager to be able to experience empathy.

Empathy is normally voiced as 'putting yourself in my shoes' or 'see it from my point of view...'. Some people become so involved with themselves that they are unwilling to ever view the world from the other person's side.

Domestic relationships and arguments in so many cases could be solved by both parties looking at their dispute from the other person's viewpoint. It is so easy to do when one asks oneself: 'Why did he say that?' or 'Why did she say that?' You see, what normally happens is that people react to the words and, of course, to the facial expression, but they don't delve into what *caused* the other person to say those words.

Empathy does not mean one has to agree with the other person. Empathy is understanding why the other person says or does what they do. There are those, as we have said, who have no empathy, and then there are those who have too much empathy, which can cause timidity, lack of assertiveness and is expressed by what we would call a lack of confidence. Empathy is no different to the normal distribution curve of life – both extremes limit success.

So what are the outward signs of the unmotivated person?

Outward Signs

Firstly, appearance. People take less care of their hair, they don't make an effort with their clothes – they get pressed and washed less frequently – shoes have an uncared-for look. And people either put on weight or lose weight. This is why it is so important for leaders to be appraising continually in the endeavour to spot any signs.

This can also be widened to the state in which they keep their car and then even to the way they work and the state of their desk or office. Finally, this uncared-for appearance can also be seen in their home.

Their facial expression will have the corners of their mouth turning down instead of up and will convey the body language messages that the brain inside the body may be unhappy, demotivated, unsure or even bitter. Such people are also more likely to experience illness.

And then the most important indicator is, of course, what people say. When they start to speak, they instantly give the listener, if they really listen to what is being said, the final indication of the motivated or unmotivated person.

Now let's look at some of the principal causes of demotivation at work.

A Lack of Confidence

This can often be expressed by the internal feeling of 'Can I do it?' or 'I'm not good enough', 'I'm unqualified, unable...', and so on.

When people lack confidence, it is primarily caused by one of the three following factors:

1. Their confidence has been removed by what somebody else has said – we will look in more detail at this under the third demotivator.
2. It may have been caused by childhood conditioning. Every baby born into the world arrives with a positive brain and during the first few months of its life receives positive input from its parents. As soon as the child starts to move, the positive inputs increase, the 'Yes, you can's, the 'You can do it's. The infant is soon able to stand, the pride of the parents increases and so do the positives.

    Eventually, the first steps are taken. The baby can walk, friends and family are quite naturally invited to share in the pleasure, but as soon as the baby is really able to walk, the inputs can turn dramatically from positive to negative – 'Be careful', 'Don't do that', 'Don't touch, you might hurt yourself'... and so that positive brain starts to experience NO–NO conditioning.
3. By past experience conditioning.

Successful experience	Failure
↓	↓
Confidence	Lack of confidence
↓	↓
I can	I can't

Suppose you are asked to make a speech. Your subconscious will automatically go to recall. If the last speech you gave went down well, the 'Yes I can do it' will come to the forefront. If the last speech was a disaster, then your past experience conditioning will be providing you with the 'I can't' feeling. This, of course, can be overcome, as you will see; but what is important here is to understand how you feel. If you have never given a speech before then your subconscious recall will be saying 'Can I do it?'

It is therefore essential that, in managing oneself as well as others, you firstly try to understand the causes that create this lack of confidence. And secondly that you do not become the cause for future lack of confidence. Everybody from time to time if they are doing something new will experience a confidence shake-up. If somebody ever says they never lack confidence it means they are never doing anything new.

An effective manager must therefore not destroy the confidence in others as this will most certainly demotivate. This will also create a loss of trust and loyalty. In Chapter 5 we will look and see how to build greater confidence.

Worry

The word 'worry' comes from the Anglo Saxon word 'weirgan' which means to strangle, to choke until there is no life left. Worry can almost do that to some people. Worry is, of course, a factor of demotivation. It is the feeling that people have when they worry about what will happen if they fail; the fear that if they make a mistake they could lose their job; and perhaps the most obnoxious fear is that of being ridiculed in front of one's colleagues or peers.

In some organizations the worry linked to the fear of making a mistake causes the safety and security of no action and certainly no decision making. It is the feeling of 'What happens if I fail?' – it is, in some cases, the fear that I'm going to be criticized in public. As I have already said, it is so important for managers to prevent this culture of worry, as this in turn can lead to people not sleeping well and having a distressing private life.

It is essential for progress and survival for people to make decisions and if decisions are going to be taken, a percentage of those will almost certainly result in mistakes. A motivational management style will never demotivate an individual by punishing that person for a mistake.

All the great leaders and entrepreneurs in the world readily admit they make mistakes and errors of judgement. They are just fortunate that the right decisions outweigh the wrong ones.

Leaders will develop a total understanding and a passionate belief that failure is not a person but is an unattractive result. It is of course a change of emphasis – making it clear that, although the results are failing, the people are not failures.

Negative Opinions

This surely has to be the single and most evil demotivator. It is what other people say that does the harm; and if I were to pick out the single most damaging habit that humanity is guilty of, it would be that of negative communication. More success, and potential success, has been destroyed by the negative opinion of people than by any other single factor.

Within any organization, if one person becomes negative it spreads almost like a forest fire and everybody becomes negative. Any person who is unable or unwilling to understand fully the danger and effect of negative opinion will never be able to master motivation.

This is a cancer, and I use the word with all the awareness of its horrendous connotations. It is the harmfulness of what people say to each other; the criticizing, condemning and complaining; the moaning, the griping, the unkind gossip and the negative rumour. Have you noticed that the grapevine in business very rarely produces healthy fruit? It is always diseased.

A negative group or team becomes an unproductive group or team. A negative person loses their productive capability. This really is such a destroyer of potential success and achievement that you MUST understand what is meant by negative talk, comment or communication in any form. Understanding is essential in order for you to be in a position to either prevent or deal with this horrible human characteristic.

Firstly, differentiate between constructive and destructive criticism – welcome the former and ban the latter (make sure, of course, that you practise what you preach). Secondly, create an environment where people will come to you or will attend meetings with ideas about 'HOW TO' rather than 'HOW NOT TO'. Thirdly, make sure you have prevented a negative culture by training your people in the effects of negative communication. Fourthly, make sure you and your people are equipped to deal with a negative outbreak if it should occur. Stock up with 'ZAPANEG' the negativity repellent (available from RDO – see details at back of book).

Suppose you have a good idea and you discuss your good idea with a friend and this individual gives you negative feedback. Your idea won't work, it is not the right time, you wouldn't be able to carry it out anyhow... How do you feel? Motivated or demotivated? You know the answer and so do I.

Firstly let me ask that if you ever seek an opinion or advice from another person, are they the best possible person to give you their opinion? You can ask a taxi driver his opinion of brain surgery and no doubt he will have one but there must be some question as to the validity of that opinion. The principle must be that when opinions are given, check out their authenticity, ie whether that person has the qualifications, experience or knowledge on the subject on which they are giving an opinion. Also remember that the experts can be wrong, as shown in the fascinating book *The Experts Speak* by Christopher Cerf and Victor Navasky, published by Pantheon Books.

Edison said: 'The talking picture will not supplant the regular silent motion picture.'

Aristotle said: 'Women may be said to be an inferior man.'

'For the majority of people, smoking has a beneficial effect': Dr Ian McDonald, surgeon, quoted in Newsweek, 18 November, 1963.

'The aeroplane will never fly': Lord Haldane, 1907.

'Television won't last – it's a flash in the pan': Mary Somerville, 1948.

The above were comments from the so-called experts. So what chance have any of us got with the bloke we meet in the pub!

Remember if you are on the receiving end of somebody else's negative opinion, it is only an opinion – they may be right or, on the other hand, they may be wrong; and it seems a characteristic of the most successful people in life that they very rarely give a straight negative opinion.

They are more likely, when passing on their advice, to look for the worst-case scenario and then, after checking all the possibilities of success, they end up by giving you more information. With this comes a greater understanding of the subject on which you want an opinion so that you are better able to form your own opinion and make your own decision.

While on the subject of opinions, new and aspiring politicians should learn how to use the word 'never' – and then never say never.

A Feeling of 'No Future Here'

When anyone feels that they have no future they are, of course, going to be demotivated. In some businesses people have to wait for the clichéd 'dead man's shoes'. In other cases, they know there is no chance of promotion as this will go to a member of the ruling family.

In some organizations advancement is determined by the number of years of service, while in other companies all the senior positions are filled from outside.

It must be accepted that it is not necessarily bad practice for businesses not to provide a career path. In many cases people will use their employers as stepping stones to their own objective, which, of course, is perfectly healthy and understandable.

What is right is that both the employer and employee should be able to recognize and respect their own terms or position of employment. The 'no future here' feeling can be managed and diminished by good management. If the manager is aware that there may not be career advancements or opportunities within their organization they can at least provide the stimulus and motivation that reduces that no-future-here feeling. They can do this by providing recognition for jobs done well, by changing and sharing responsibilities, by involvement in decision making and, perhaps most importantly, by providing training opportunities.

It is obvious (but nevertheless must be said) that it would be demotivational to provide training for skills that could never be used within that organization.

I Feel Unimportant

When a person genuinely feels unimportant they will, of course, be demotivated. This can also be expressed as 'Nobody cares about me', 'I am insignificant', 'I am but a little cog in this large machine'.

This can – like all the demotivators – be so easily prevented by good management. Line managers with leadership and motivational skills know that recognition can remove this feeling. It can be just a 'thank you'; it can be the personal letter from the senior manager of a management team; it can be as simple as the chairman of the company knowing and using the individual's name.

There is a lovely example of a person visiting a building site. On speaking to one bricklayer he asked him what he was doing, to which the bricklayer replied: 'I am laying bricks'. The second bricklayer was asked the same question, to which he replied: 'I am building a wall', and the third bricklayer responded to that same question with: 'I am building a house'.

The third bricklayer obviously felt he was part of the project and he most certainly felt very important.

This is why management style has gone from the 'Big is Beautiful' syndrome to 'Small is Beautiful'. Perhaps the simplest and easiest way of removing this feeling of unimportance is to take active steps instantly to give instead of take. Look to see what you can do for another person – how can you help them?

'You can get what you want if you help enough other people to get what they want.'

'I Don't Know What's Going On'

This is such a common demotivator when people feel, rightly or wrongly, that they don't know what's going on – nobody bothers to tell them anything, they are always the last to hear.

In an organization where this is a common feeling, information is often communicated via the proverbial grapevine. This information in most cases is frighteningly inaccurate, and is virtually always negative and distorted by gossip.

This can all be summed up as poor communication. For many years British managers stopped talking to their workforce and communicated only through the trade unions. What an extraordinary way to manage, motivate and communicate with one's employees! Unions, of course, have a rightful place in a healthy society, but their role is not to communicate between the management and their employees. Again, prevention is so easy. People should be kept informed, they should hear the news from their own bosses and they shouldn't have to know what's going on by reading the national press. They should not have to be dependent on rumour. As we all know, rumour is invariably inaccurate.

People Are Rewarded Not For What They Do, But For Who They Are

Under the laws of motivation we discussed the importance of recognition in the motivation stakes. In any organization where people are promoted, rewarded or recognized for being a member of the right family or due to a personal relationship or even just because 'their face fits', then demotivation will be the effect.

Here is a list of questions exploring the causes of demotivation; fill it in and assess your own organization.

	Yes	No
Is the company policy acceptable?		
Does everyone know the policy?		
Is the policy right for customers?		
Are the core processes suitable for delivery of customer care?		
Is there job security?		
Are relations good with all personnel and management?		
Are work hours impacting on family and home life?		
Do people/you feel valued at work?		

In order to make use of what you have read about in this chapter, write out your own list of things that really demotivate you. Devise a strategy that will cure or prevent demotivation, carry it out, then put the plan away in a drawer for six months. After this time has elapsed, check it again to make sure that all the problems are still being dealt with.

Lack of Training

The second most common cause of people needing medical treatment for stress is lack of training. With ever increasing demands for change, people at work are given new responsibilities and new tasks. They are then expected by their managers to carry out tasks according to the managers' expectations, but they are not trained or given guidance. They don't do the job because they don't know how to do it, or they don't do it because of the fear of getting it wrong. They then try to hide the situation and, as a result, feel terribly guilty. Leaders on the other hand will never delegate without fully understanding the consequences, and will also passionately embrace the culture of investing in their people – training and helping them to make sure that those tasks will lead to success.

Pocket Reminders

Understand and avoid the demotivators:

- Lack of confidence
- Worry
- Negative opinions
- A feeling of 'no future here'
- Feeling unimportant
- Not knowing what is going on
- False recognition
- Lack of training

Stock up with neg repellent

Wise Words

One of the easiest ways to be right is to predict failure, especially for yourself.

4

Assertiveness

Assertiveness is a little like motivation inasmuch as many people feel they should be more assertive or that they are just not assertive enough. Many people seem to want it, but are not quite sure what it really is.

Assertion is probably best described as expressing opinions, thoughts and feelings in a non-defensive manner – clearly and openly. It is being able to make requests and to refuse requests that are unacceptable. This sounds simple enough, but in reality many people experience great difficulty in refusing other people's demands as well as in communicating with friends, colleagues or – more often – people at work. Assertion does not mean being heavy-handed, dogmatic, boring or over-bearing.

In the previous chapter we looked at the importance of empathy and of understanding self-confidence. Empathy has to play a major part in being assertive. Assertiveness involves communicating in a way that takes account of other people's feelings. It also has to be an expression of self-confidence.

In Chapter 5, where we look at the technique necessary to motivate oneself, I also look at a few ideas on how to build self-confidence. It is a lack of self-confidence that causes people to feel that they are not sufficiently assertive.

Fear of Rejection

People who genuinely feel that their style of communication is too submissive and not assertive enough often find that the cause is due to past experience. The cause in many cases is past feelings of rejection – or what the individual may term as rejection. In reality, they are often mistaken.

In its most simple definition, rejection is when the person to whom one is communicating replies with or implies the word 'no'. Please do accept that when anybody says 'no' to you it is only ever 'no' at that particular time. It is not 'no' later in the day, tomorrow, next week, next month or next year.

> Let me ask you a simple and straightforward question. Do you own, or have you bought, or even have you done something that previously you have said 'no' to?
> I guarantee your reply will be 'yes'.

You see, our circumstances change. Our hopes, demands and aspirations are continually on the move and we all change our minds. 'No' is not a rejection; it is just a 'no' for whatever reason at that moment in time.

Developing Assertiveness

Many people feel that to develop their assertiveness they need to be more aggressive. The human race reacts very badly to aggression and rejects it, so this feeling cannot be right.

Assertion is an interpersonal skill. It can reflect your habitual way of thinking. It can project your innermost feelings about yourself and, of course, your relationships with others.

I have already said that being assertive means that one should communicate clearly, openly and non-defensively. Don't make apologies for yourself unless they are absolutely genuinely due.

I am sure you have got friends who have said to you, 'Oh, I couldn't ask that'. But why not? Or 'I couldn't say that to her...' Why not?

The balance that is so important is that between empathy and expressing your opinions and feelings. Remember, you may be right, but equally, you may be wrong.

So let's look at nine steps that help the individual to develop their assertiveness.

1. Expect to be anxious

It is quite normal and totally acceptable in the field of human communication that everybody, from time to time, feels anxious when they say what they think or feel, and if any individual honestly says they never feel anxious, they must have no understanding, empathy or feelings about anybody else.

So don't be embarrassed. Your anxious feeling is totally acceptable – it is because you care.

2. Build your confidence

We will be covering the techniques for this in Chapter 5. Suffice to say here that confidence can be like a habit – bad habits take time to develop and are created by continual practice and repetition until at some stage they become hard to lose. **But they do take time to develop fully.**

Good habits are exactly the same. They take time to form and must be continually practised. **Good habits, when they come to fruition, are just as difficult to get out of.**

3. Believe in yourself

If you do not already fully believe in yourself, then start NOW! Because if you don't believe in yourself, you are making it very hard for anybody else to do so. What I mean by this is the way you speak to yourself! The 'Yes I can', the 'I am able'. It is so important that you can say to yourself: 'How do I feel about myself? What is my self-image?' Remember, you are completely in control.

If you think you are beaten, you are
If you think you are not, you don't
If you'd like to win but think you can't
It's almost certain you won't
Life's battles don't always go
To the stronger or faster person
But sooner or later the person who wins
Is the person who thinks they can

Anon

4. Watch and listen to what others communicate to you

'Watch' means be aware of body language. The signals that are conveyed by a person's body language can provide a great deal of information. There are approximately 750,000 body language signals, some of which are very difficult to control. These signals will invariably give you more accurate information than what somebody actually says.

Being assertive does not mean just getting your viewpoint across. It is a combination of being able to listen and persuade. As all salespeople know, these are essential ingredients when selling your ideas.

Perhaps one of the keys to being more assertive is to understand, then know through belief, how easy it is to sell one's ideas. In my book *Selling To Win*, I cover in great detail the systems and methodology of persuasion. Though intentionally written for those selling products and services, it is a book that everybody should read, as everybody is selling something to somebody – and there is such a great difference between telling and selling.

In developing this stage of your assertiveness self-training, practise listening to another person's viewpoint without submissively surrendering your own.

Let me remind you again: ask yourself 'Why did he say that?' or 'Why did she say that?'

5. Consider the situation

This means that, in order to communicate effectively and assertively, give yourself time to think and consider the situation that needs to be handled. It will strengthen your confidence and your ability to communicate your message.

> There is that lovely expression: 'Act in haste, repent at leisure.'

Everybody has a right to consider before responding, and in helping yourself to develop the right thought process, try thinking what the end result is you want to achieve. In so much poor communication, people try to score points or to win an argument. In the sales world, the saying is: 'You can win the argument, but you lose the sale.'

So why score points? Decide the result that you want and this will help you to think about a positive solution. Good thinking means the brain should be allowed to be flexible. Don't allow your thinking process to become entrenched, as it will be difficult to think in any other way.

6. Plan your response

When thinking about a situation that needs resolving, be sure to check that the problem you are solving is the important issue and not just a smokescreen hiding the real crux of the matter.

So, in planning your response, decide when and how you will make it. In your mental preparation, come to terms with yourself and accept the fact that in some instances others involved could get upset or angry.

Don't just expect the best outcome – mentally prepare for the worst-case scenario; what is the worst that could happen? I might add that this very rarely comes to pass. A truly positive thinking person always plans for the best, clearly has in their mind a positive result, but has also looked at the worst possible result and has a contingency plan just in case. Having mentally prepared for the worst possible result, it is then deleted from the thought process of the positive thinker's mind.

7. Make your point

If, for some extraordinary reason, you get very nervous or you feel very anxious, take a couple of deep breaths. This normally settles the nervous system, generating oxygen in the bloodstream. Relax and see clearly in your mind's eye a positive result. In making your point, let me emphasize once again – be absolutely clear in what you are saying.

Be open and non-defensive. Do not imagine that the other person is tuned in to your level of thinking. Do not rely upon their imagination and don't communicate with the feeling, 'Well, I hope they get the message'.

There must be no misunderstanding and, of course, no sarcasm. In getting your point of view across effectively, please accept that, to a certain extent, person-to-person communication is a sales process. Its aim is to persuade somebody to see clearly the result of what you wish to achieve.

The steps necessary to achieve this result are never as important as communicating a clear picture of what the result could be like.

8. No nicely

This is probably the most important characteristic of an assertive person – being able to say no nicely. It appears that a lack of assertiveness is more common in women than it is in men. I am not sure whether this is actually the case, or whether women are just more honest and more prepared to accept this as a possible weakness in their character. I am sure in reality there are just as many males who get what can be described as sat on or overburdened. But the real skill is being able to and willing to know when it is right to say no – and, equally, to be able to say no in a friendly, logical and positive manner.

9. Be positive

Finally, ALWAYS BE POSITIVE – happy, cheerful and smiling. People who communicate with a cheerful and positive expression somehow always seem to get their message across.

Say something nice, not creepy – a general compliment, for example. Be willing to give praise and do so enthusiastically. People will feel safer with you when they know how you really feel – remember, if we don't stand for something, we'll fall for anything.

Pocket Reminders

The nine steps to increasing assertiveness:

1. Expect to be anxious
   ↓
2. Build your confidence
   ↓
3. Believe in yourself
   ↓
4. Watch and listen
   ↓
5. Consider the situation
   ↓
6. Plan your response
   ↓
7. Make your point
   ↓
8. No nicely
   ↓
9. BE POSITIVE!

Wise Words

When a person lowers their voice, they want something.
When they raise it, it is a sign they didn't get it.

Motivating Yourself by Building Your Own Confidence

The most valuable asset for most people is also the least valued. It is an asset that, with the right care, can appreciate dramatically. It is an asset that is taken for granted and that is impossible to put a price on. This asset, of course, is one's brain and the thinking processes that accompany it.

Imagine a computer created and constructed by the most brilliant technologically advanced brains of the world. The computer is so vast that its capacity is the size of the new Wembley Stadium. The computer would cost billions and billions of pounds, yet every individual has a computer that is more powerful than any mankind will ever create.

Researchers continually tell us that only a small proportion of the human brain is still understood and used. The greatest development as we proceed through the 21st century will be a greater understanding and fuller usage of the brain.

So why is this relevant to self-motivation? Because very simply there has to be a direct corollary between self-belief and personal motivation.

If you can accept that your most valuable asset is your brain, it is then worthwhile accepting some basic principles on its function. For example, whatever you put in, you will get back out. The brain operates in a similar fashion to the modern computer. The brain, moreover, has the powers of reason and creativity that the computer does not.

So, if you accept that the brain is the most incredible storage area, it then becomes essential to take care in what you are asking it to store. Some people will have a brain filled full of negative thoughts and experiences. They will continually input the 'I can't's and reams of excuses as to why they are unable to do things.

So when confronted with a new opportunity or challenge, their brains, on being asked a question, will deliver a negative answer.

In the chapter on assertiveness, we discussed the importance of building confidence. Let's now touch on the six steps necessary to build that confidence and, in turn, build the self-belief which can become the foundation for inner self-motivation.

1. Get rid of excuses

So many people hold themselves back by making unjustifiable and largely untrue excuses to themselves, such as:

▓ 'I can't.'
▓ 'I am unable to because...'
▓ 'I haven't had the right education.'
▓ 'I am not assertive enough.'
▓ 'I am too old.'
▓ 'I am too young.'
▓ 'I suffer from poor health.'
▓ 'I am not lucky.'
▓ 'I'm never in the right place at the right time.'
▓ 'I didn't go to the right schools.'
▓ 'It's my family background.'
▓ 'I was born under the wrong birth sign.'

Excuses. You can find an excuse for almost anything, so in

building confidence, never, and I mean never, make an excuse. It may be very convenient, and I do accept at times it can be reassuring, but excuses hold people back from goal achievement.

So try to eradicate from your thoughts and vocabulary the words I CAN'T and I AM NOT and replace them with I CAN and I AM.

Remember, your brain is a storage area – what you put in, you will in turn get back out, so replace the negative insertions with the positive.

2. Use picture power

Firstly, let me ask you two questions. How do you feel about yourself? What is your own self-image?

I hope that you will be able to answer by saying that you are proud of yourself, you feel good about yourself – but you would like to be better.

We have all heard the expression 'Seeing is believing.' The brain, with its limitless capacities, can help you immeasurably to achieve life's ambitions if you give it the chance. Picture yourself as the person you want to be. Clearly visualize whatever it is you want to achieve. The more you think about it, the greater the certainty will be of a positive result.

There is another expression that says: 'What we think about, we become.' I remember saying this once in one of my lectures, whereupon a man shouted out from the audience: 'But I don't want to be a girl'! But seriously though, this can work in a negative way as well as a positive one.

If you continually allow your thoughts to dwell on illnesses and bad health, you almost certainly will experience the ailments that you think about. If you continually think about negative results in your relationship or business career, they will come to fruition.

So in building confidence by using the brain's picture-power image process, it is essential to make sure that what you are thinking and vividly seeing is positive. It must be conducive to your own self-image and its improvement, and your thoughts must be towards your goals, aspirations and happiness in life.

Think about what you want, not what you don't want. Go to sleep thinking positive ideas. Create positive images of successful experiences, and endeavour to make this a habit. This 'picture power' involves visualizing; your brain is used to doing this, as it regularly visualizes future happenings. The great sportspeople of the world concentrate on the result before an event, attempting to remove all distractions from the mind. You should do a similar thing; from today, get into the habit of visualizing the positive and expect the best.

So what happens if you catch yourself thinking a negative thought?

Let me ask you, what do you do when your film has been processed and you are looking at the prints and find that one is out of focus or the light has got in and it's a lousy picture? May I suggest that you will almost certainly discard that print. Your brain will operate in exactly the same way.

If you catch yourself thinking a thought that is not conducive to your goal, say to yourself: 'I'm not going to think that. I don't want to think that.' Tell your brain in your own words to get rid of that thought and instantly replace it with a more positive one. Remember, as I have already said, during your waking hours, you control what your brain thinks about. It does not control you.

3. Don't fear failure

Fear of failure reduces confidence and quite naturally self-motivation too.

When facing a new opportunity or challenge, ask yourself what is the worst that can happen, and what might be termed as failure. Let me remind you again, failure is not a person, only an unsavoury result.

The danger with a lot of positive thinking training is that some people can become unbearably and unrealistically positive – so heavenly minded that they are no earthly good.

A good balance is essential. One must be realistic: having looked at the worst-case scenario and thought about how to handle a situation should it arise – in other words, having planned a contingency – remove that thought completely and concentrate on your plan for success.

But whatever you do, don't fear failure. This holds so many people back from ever trying, doing or achieving because they are unable to come to terms with the possibility that they might fail.

Some people actually never try anything because this fear of failure has been cultivated in their brain for years. They think about it daily so they never actually do anything and in turn become unconfident, unsure and unhappy. Let me remind you of that wonderful quote: 'The only way to conquer fear is to keep doing the thing you fear to do.'

Before leaving the subject of failure, there are some people who are motivated by the fear of failure. While they are motived by the fear, they never visualize themselves actually failing, and that is the crucial difference.

4. Appearance builds confidence

I have discussed this topic already in this book and I make no apology for repeating it. You must take continual account of your personal appearance.

Have you ever been to an evening engagement where everybody apart from yourself was dressed in dinner jacket or evening dress? If you haven't, no doubt you have a fear that you might. If it were to happen, you would experience a confidence crisis. It would be the same brain, the same body, but your outward appearance would have let you down. You must understand the importance of outer appearance and spend money to make sure it is looking good, so that the inside has a chance to become good. But, like everything else, be realistic. Some people over-indulge in their appearance and end up only feeding their own ego.

May I remind you of the expression: 'The bigger the ego, the smaller the bank balance.'

5. Compile a record of past successes

Everybody has successes in their lives. Equally, everybody has down spells when they either lose confidence or experience a reversal of their pattern of success. When this happens, it should be the responsibility of the individual to bounce back again.

A good idea is to compile a record of past success. Think back to your earliest memory of success. It may be at your first school, winning the egg and spoon race. It may be the congratulations received on a drawing or painting. But from that earliest memory, recall every success experience you have had in your life. This could be captured verbally on an audio cassette or CD or compiled in the form of a scrap book. Whatever method used, add to it every bit of success that comes your way. Then, when later faced with a possible loss of confidence, you can turn to that record and refresh your most valuable asset with the memory of some of those success experiences. This will diminish the feeling of self-doubt or loss of confidence that circumstances have provoked.

Motivation can only perpetuate on the back of hope. To motivate oneself, one has to have hope. Hope, of course, is looking forward to the future. Therefore, for individuals to motivate themselves, they must be responsible for creating their own hope. Truly self-motivated individuals do not allow their hope to be out of their control or provided by others – by the government, by the world political scene, by the weather or any other factor that is not in their direct control.

So let's now run through the steps necessary to create hope and be focused. For the brain to operate, it must be given goals, so the following chapter reveals the stages for setting goals in life.

Pocket Reminders

The six steps to building your confidence:

1. Get rid of excuses
   ↓
2. Use picture power
   ↓
3. Don't fear failure
   ↓
4. Consider your appearance
   ↓
5. Keep a record of past successes
   ↓
6. Be a positive realist

Wise Words

The more we do something good, the less praise we get for it. The more we do something bad, the more punishment we receive.

How to Motivate Yourself by Setting Goals

Setting Your Goals

The extraordinary thing about goals is that so few people actually do decide what they want. You've no doubt heard the expression: 'A person who is going nowhere normally gets there.' But it seems quite extraordinary when you ask people what they want, how few really do *know* what they want. People talk in glib terms of 'I want to be successful' or 'I'd like to be a millionaire' or 'I want happiness'. But they actually don't know what they really want and then are unhappy and negative because they haven't got it.

What the mind can accurately conceive and believe, it is forced to achieve. The history of mankind has been a history of goal achievement. Leading psychologists now regard the brain and the nervous system as highly complex automatic goal-seeking mechanisms. So we all have the equipment necessary to achieve what we really want if we care to use it. And if you want something badly enough and you have the equipment that will help you to get it, make use of it!

So here are the stages of goal setting and of achievement.

1. List your desires

Make a list of all the things you really want, both long term and short term, in your business life and in your private life, both tangible and intangible.

In making this list, be realistic. I have heard motivational speakers say to their audiences: 'Set big goals.' They are wrong. And it can be dangerous. It may sound highly motivational in a convention hall, but the danger is that short-term goals that are too big don't become believable and are not achieved. The goal setter then becomes demotivated and, in some cases, never tries again. Big goals *can* be set long term. They should be staged and there is nothing wrong whatsoever in enlarging the size of one's thinking to become a 'big thinking' person. Let me remind you once again: **we become what we think about.**

Don't put down certain items on your goal sheet because you think you ought to. The only thoughts you put down should be the ones that you really, really, *really* want.

Don't just put down monetary goals. They must be turned into something tangible unless they are the removal of a debt. Money is required to be spent on something specific that you want and should not be an end in itself.

Making your list can be a lot of fun but it's a serious business. Compiling this list is something that should be completely private unless you have a very close relationship with another person, in which case one's goals should be shared and discussed. Many marriages or relationships break up because the two people involved have different goals. It is quite extraordinary how few people do spend any time in thinking about what they *really* want to do, achieve or experience in their life.

Having said that, there is of course the exception. In the UK, Wednesday and Saturday nights are, for many, the only time when what could loosely be described as goals are discussed. This is the few minutes prior to the National Lottery draw, and the conversations go something like this:

'Supposing we win £7 million?'

'No, we don't need all of that, but £1 million would be quite nice, and if we were to win a million – well, we would buy a new house, a new car, have an incredible holiday and, of course, we would give quite a bit to charity' (hoping this might increase their chances!).

The balls go into the machine, the numbers are announced and the conversation finishes with the words 'well, we got two this week – better than last week'. Yes, of course, the lottery can be a bit of fun, but one should never depend for one second upon the odds of winning – which are, apparently, 14 million to one. But when people select their goals, they are clearly defined, really wanted and the odds are evens – you can't get much better than that.

When making up your list, the keyword is REALLY.

2. Select a goal

Now select from your list of goals a primary one, taking into account these three points that are so important to remember:

(a) It should be high enough to be worth the effort.
(b) It should be achievable in months, not years, and ideally within a maximum of three months.

   It must be something you can reach quite quickly. As we all know, success breeds success. It will build your confidence and will prove that the system works for you. But above everything else, the human brain is more responsive to the immediate short term than the longer term.
(c) Be realistic about any financial considerations if money is involved.

3. Define your target

Define your chosen goal in complete detail. At this stage of goal setting, it is important for your most valuable asset to be focused and to by crystal clear as to what the goal is. Your goal might be that you'd like to lose weight, but losing weight is not a goal. Be specific – how much weight exactly do you want to lose? The goal may be: 'I would like to be fitter.' Exactly what does fitness mean for that individual? It may mean being able to do 20 press-ups and run two miles.

Your target, therefore, must be totally quantifiable and measurable. Another goal might be: 'I would like to be promoted.' Promoted to what? What position, what title, what responsibility, etc? For somebody else, it may be that they would like a new car. Is the car to be new or second hand? Which make and model, what colour and which extras? Let me remind you of the saying: 'What the mind of man can accurately conceive and believe, it is forced to achieve.'

4. Use your subconscious

Imagine that you have achieved your goal. Again, we are talking about using your most valuable asset. Let your conscious and subconscious mind vividly imagine being in the position of attaining your goal. Over the years, I have trained a lot of people in public speaking and so many of the delegates on my courses have come saying to themselves: 'I am a bad speaker.' One of the first stages of becoming a good speaker is to reverse that infusion of negativity by saying 'I am a good speaker' and clearly imagining the success of each speaking opportunity.

This may all sound very trite, and I have had many people on my personal development courses question this stage. Your subconscious is more powerful than your conscious mind. Let your subconscious take over by clearly visualizing what it is you really want to achieve. Your subconscious will bring it to fruition. How can I imagine I've gained something before I have? Who's kidding who? All I can say is that this is not some strange technique that I personally have dreamt up. It is one of the greatest principles of all personal development and success. Let your brain take an active part in the stages towards your goal achievement: it is the great spectrum of visualization. Dr Roger Bannister, the first man in the world to run a mile in under four minutes, visualized running four quarter-miles and each quarter-mile was under a minute.

One day I phoned a good friend and business colleague, Frank Tijou, whom I hadn't seen for some months. My first question, quite naturally, was to ask how he was, to which he replied that he had just been told he had cancer. I personally was devastated as I thought that he, as I am sure we have all said at some stage, was the last person I would have thought to have this debilitating disease. I then enquired as to where he had the cancer, and he replied that he had cancer of the lymph glands.

I was certainly no authority on this subject, but I had been told that this is one of the most serious cancers. In my shock I asked him how he felt, to which he replied: 'Great!' This 'great' was almost bellowed down the phone. He then went on to say that he had six chemotherapy treatments to go through, he would lose all his hair and he would feel dreadfully ill shortly after each treatment. He would allow himself a short time to stay at home to overcome the sickness – but he had got a very busy period in front of him. After the final treatment there would be a period when he would have to wait for the final check-up and then he and his wife, Kate, were having a holiday in Turkey.

Frank and Kate had their holiday and he went on to achieve many years of success at work and great joy in his personal life. The combination of brilliant medical help, the visualization and the power of the subconscious mind were all factors that led to such a positive outcome and proved to be too powerful for Frank's cancer.

Your brain can become your greatest ally and supporter. It can be your greatest fan if you give it a chance. It will most certainly be your most productive employee if you give it the right training. Continuing this analogy, some people think their brain is their most expensive employee, as it always thinks the worst, makes all the excuses and continually sees the negative rather than the positive.

5. Set a deadline

Now set a deadline for your goal's achievement. Decide the exact date by which you want that goal. We all respond to deadlines. If we know a plane is leaving at a certain time, we make an effort to catch it. So you must decide when you want to achieve your goal.

Isn't it funny how, every year, people say that they will do their Christmas shopping earlier, or even do it during the year? But every year, Christmas shopping seems to be done by the vast majority in the last two weeks. The human brain does respond to deadlines!

6. Carry a reminder

Carry your goals. Every person who is ambitious and striving for achievement should carry their goals with them as a reminder and a purpose. I have already said that life is not one amazing upward trend of achievement. We all have our ups and downs, our good days and bad days. Very few people have to learn how to cope with success, and when you have experienced success, you will quite naturally be more motivated by it.

If you ever find that you are distracted or you experience a setback or perhaps – even more commonly – somebody else tries to deflect you from your goals, you may find it useful to have a copy of your goals on your person – either written in a diary or on a card – to act as a constant reminder. **This helps you to remember your purpose.**

Many yachts are sailing the oceans of the world right now without a helmsman. The sails are preset, the self-steering gear is in operation and the yachts will invariably be on course for their destination.

Robin Fielder, my ex-partner and co-founder of Leadership Development, tells the story that when he was sailing out of Hayling Island with a visitor on his yacht, his guest asked him: 'How come there are some yachts sailing north and some yachts sailing south yet the wind is coming from one direction, the east?' And he replied:

It is not the direction of the wind that is important, it is the set of the sails.

And so it is with goal achievement and self-motivation: the stages are essential.

Your Personal Plan

This now leads to the final part of goal setting and achievement. What we have done so far is build the stages of deciding what you really want and training the brain to become your most effective and profitable employee. The final stage is to prepare a plan.

Following on from our nautical analogy, imagine a cruise liner leaving from a UK port on a journey to Sydney, Australia. One day out from the home port a passenger asks the Captain 'Which route are we taking?', to which the Captain replies 'Now that's an interesting question. We could, of course, go the long way round or, on the other hand, we could take the short route through the Suez Canal. That is an interesting question. I'll find out.'

Now this is a really positive passenger who follows this question with another, 'Well, Captain, I look forward to hearing that. But tell me, where will our first port of call be, as no doubt we will require some more fuel and possibly food and I would like to send some postcards', to which the Captain again replies 'That is an interesting question. You are right, we will have to stop off somewhere. Don't worry, I will make a phone call and find out.'

Of course, this is a farcical situation, as in the real world the owners of the liner, having decided the destination and the date of departure, etc, would have prepared a master plan for the conduct of that voyage. The route would have been decided, as well as stopping-off points, the number of crew, the tonnage of fuel and food, the number of tickets that needed to be sold and the agencies that would have been employed to sell them. Every single detail would have been planned well in advance.

The same must be done for your life and your goals. The liner, without its master plan, would almost certainly have become shipwrecked on some rocks. So in preparing the plan for your own goals, the simple stages are these: Take a sheet of paper, write the exact goal at the top with the date of its required achievement and then make a list of all the stages necessary. An example is given on the next page.

I accept that this may take just a little bit of effort, and perhaps even a little bit of thought and work, but it is your goal and it is your life. Is it worth it?

Having completed the plan, now all you have to do is concentrate on the first stage and, when that is completed, go on to the next stage. Each stage of the plan should have its own dated deadline. What we have done is to break that goal down into a series of small easily manageable and even more believable simple steps, using one of those great principles from the eight laws of success that says:

SUCCESS BY THE INCH IS A CINCH
AND BY THE YARD IT'S HARD

GOAL: To lose 14 lbs **Start date:** _____	**Goal date:** _____
Action plan	*Action date*
Have complete doctor's health check	_____
Select suitable diet	_____
Purchase diet plan provisions	_____
Start exercise plan:	
Week 1 Lose 2lbs	_____
Week 2 Lose 2lbs (4lbs)	_____
Week 3 Lose 2lbs (6lbs)	_____
Week 4 Lose 2lbs (8lbs)	_____
Week 5 Lose 2lbs (10lbs)	_____
Week 6 Lose 2lbs (12lbs)	_____
Week 7 Lose 2lbs (14lbs)	_____

The above is a simple plan. Concentrate on one stage at a time and tick off each stage when it is achieved.

This is the formula for goal achievement. It is infallible and relies on simple common sense, so why doesn't everybody get what they want in life? There are three very simple reasons:

1. They don't believe they can because of life's negative conditioning.
2. They haven't been shown how.
3. They don't really want to, and therefore aren't prepared to pay the price of a little bit of work or effort in order to achieve their goals.

> Zig Ziggler, perhaps the greatest motivator, makes the point that you do not pay the price for success, but enjoy the benefits.

Let's now move on to a few more ideas that help towards the building of self-motivation.

Right Place, Right Time

Some people convince themselves that they are just not lucky. However, it must be remembered that there is a great difference between luck and chance. Chance is the lottery win or the horse that comes in first. Luck is something that the majority of us can control.

So many successful people often say 'Well, I've been lucky' or 'I've had a stroke of luck', but this invariably comes down to being in the right place at the right time. In order to be in the right place at the right time that individual has most certainly done something to be there. They were not just sitting at home hoping to become lucky.

Luck is best broken down into the mnemonic:

Labour
Under
Correct
Knowledge

Labour is *doing* something. The correct knowledge is knowing where you are today, knowing where you want to be and having a plan to get there. We have just covered this in goal setting and achievement.

The Right Company

In keeping yourself motivated you must be aware of the company you keep. Are the people that you meet or surround yourself with positive or negative? If you are continually mixing with negative people who are criticizing, condemning and complaining, finding fault with everything and everybody, it is almost certain that, however positive you are, you will start to conform. The reverse is also true. If you meet and circulate amongst people who are positive, enthusiastic, who have goals, they will, of course, have hope. They are most likely to be motivated.

Therefore, you must continually check who you are meeting and talking with and, in keeping your own motivational level high, avoid to the best of your ability people who are negative. Let's be realistic, it may be a close member of your family or a loved one who is negative. Ask yourself 'Why did she say that?' or 'Why did he say that?' It is the empathy–ego balance that we have already discussed. But avoid negative people wherever you can.

Self-management

Self-management does play an active part in the make-up of the self-motivated person – doing the important and often unpleasant tasks before the pleasurable ones. People sometimes described as having a weaker character than others will often have difficulty with their own self-management, and will do the jobs that please them or neglect to do the tasks that are important. I recall my mother saying to me when I was a child that the devil looks over your shoulder encouraging you and telling you to do the things you shouldn't be doing.

Perhaps a more acceptable way of communicating this principle is to use the idea that we all have two employees, **Mr Success** and **Mr Failure.**

Mr Failure will encourage you to procrastinate, to delay the things you should be doing, to put off anything that could be mildly unpleasant. Whereas Mr Success is the opposite. So fire Mr Failure!

I do ask you to consider this in some depth, as when undertaking the responsibility of managing others – be it at work or at home, and particularly with children – you must be able to manage yourself correctly and effectively. You must not fall into the trap of 'Don't do as I do, do as I say'.

But having taken steps to be more in control or to manage yourself, you should reward yourself with a treat – here we are again on the same subject of hope and having something to look forward to.

Keep yourself fit and healthy. Doctors' surgeries throughout the UK are filled with people who have no genuine illness. Their most valuable asset has become polluted. Zig Ziggler describes such behaviour as 'Stinking Thinking'.

Doesn't it seem quite extraordinary that people who are self-employed are very rarely ill and have few ailments? Why? Because they can't afford to be ill. Conversely, individuals employed by others who have little hope, few goals or aspirations and nothing to look forward to become regular visitors to the doctor's surgery and seem to suffer from every imaginable ailment.

Don't Retire

Don't retire, just at some stage stop working for a living. It is completely unnecessary to put one's brain into retirement mode, as this is not conducive to self-motivation. But on a business note, there is far too much wastage of talent, particularly in the so-called professions of accountancy and the law. Firms are set up with partners and equity partners. At a given age these people have to retire. In the vast majority of cases, this does not demonstrate a customer care culture to the clients. Relationships that have developed over many years are suddenly broken up, and the customer's contact in the firm has gone. The firm suffers because it loses an immense amount of experience. My advice is that equity partners should release their equity so that others in the firm can benefit and the firm can bring in new talent, but the partners should cut down their time at work. Maybe after a given age, they should do four days a week, then three days, two days and one day until such time as is decided. It is very difficult for the majority of people suddenly to switch from a lifetime's work to no work at all. There are of course exceptions where people have so many hobbies and interests and also sufficient income to give them great joy and fulfilment in the period of their life when they stop working for a living.

The word 'retire' is a frightening word. Countless thousands of people dedicate themselves to their employment and their company and then look forward to their retirement. Statistics show the horrifying results of how many die within one or two years of their retirement.

The retirement that they were looking forward to was a goal, and having achieved that goal there then came the vacuum with nothing to look forward to doing or achieving. They had not prepared or planned those wonderful years when they did not have to work for a living. **Nobody should ever retire, they should just stop working for a living.**

Motivate Yourself by Motivating Others

Finally, in building and maintaining one's own self-motivation, one of the greatest and finest techniques (which may sound glib, but nevertheless is emphatically true and effective) is to motivate somebody else.

As always, let's touch on the principle first that says:

WHATEVER YOU HAND OUT IN LIFE, YOU GET BACK

This law – again from the laws of success – goes on to say that there is a tenfold return.

So to motivate another person can be as simple as a smile. It is quite uncanny that while walking down a street, or even sitting in a traffic jam in your car, how a big smile offered to somebody else is returned with a smile. And isn't it hard *not* to be motivated when you are smiling? One of the great distinctions between humankind and the animal world is the ability to laugh.

Almost every problem in the world can be resolved with a sense of humour. We remove the pressures and the worry with a laugh and a joke.

Pocket Reminders

Make a detailed plan, then:

▓ Take control of your own luck
▓ Keep the right company
▓ Manage yourself
▓ Fire Mr Failure
▓ Don't retire
▓ Motivate yourself by motivating others

Wise Words

Opportunities multiply when they are seized; die when neglected.

7

Motivating the Person

Most of us at some stage in our lives are confronted with another person, who could be an employee, friend or family member, of whom we find ourselves thinking, 'If only I could motivate them. There must be something that would give them some get up and go' or 'What on earth can I do to change their attitude and get them turned on to life?'

Many managers are continually confronted with this situation – how to motivate individuals in their employ. You should always ask yourself the question, 'Why do you want to motivate that individual?' If it's a member of your family or a close friend it is normally because that person is not fulfilling their real potential. They are missing out on opportunities and are not happy or contented with themselves.

With an employee, to a certain extent, the same applies. You may believe a person has greater potential than they are exhibiting and, as an employer, it is your responsibility to maximize their potential and performance and, of course, the results of other employees.

Is the lack of motivation being caused by one of the demotivators already suggested (see Chapter 3), or is there another root cause? Ask yourself – why is he/she demotivated? And be prepared to accept the answer and possibly the blame for being the cause. If you are the cause, it is your responsibility to act – and possibly change.

It is impossible to motivate if inhibiting conditions are not conducive to motivating the person. The tragedy is that most managers won't conduct a self-inquisition because they fear the reply and won't accept that they are the cause.

Now suppose that if, after your own total self-inquisition, the lack of motivation is not caused by the environment, your management style or some of the other demotivating factors in your control, you can now move to the two fundamental stages in the theory of motivating the person:

Stage 1: Find out what they really want.
Stage 2: Show them how to get it.

What do they want?

So how do you find out what somebody really wants? The simple answer is, of course, to ask them. But let's be realistic, if you were to walk up to one of your employees and ask them in front of their workmates what they really want, one thing is sure: you are not going to get a true answer.

This should only be done in complete privacy and can normally only be approached over a period of time when the employee has developed trust in their employer or manager.

Alternatively, you can find out through observation and, of course, by listening to conversations during relaxation periods. You must accept, as we have already discussed, that a lot of people really don't know what they want and they are unhappy because they haven't got it. This leads to an inner frustration that is not conducive to being a motivated individual.

Now if somebody doesn't know what they want, it is extremely difficult to motivate them. Many young people leaving school, college or university are unsure as to what career or job they really want to get into. Many of these young people suffer enormous frustration, and in some cases a tremendous loss of self-confidence when they see their colleagues progressing and striving on in their own chosen careers.

There is no simple solution when helping somebody to find out what they really want. The common sense approach says that the caring leader or manager will help to broaden the thinking of the individual by conversation – by talking and suggesting – but this must in no way be demanding.

You must not impose your own aspirations or goals, as this becomes manipulation. In some business environments, a person's goals can be discovered by exposure to other work situations in different departments. Sometimes it may be necessary to send the person on out-placement. However, many individuals do solve this problem themselves eventually.

How can they get it?

The second stage – showing the person how to get what they really want – sounds easier than it is in reality. But once you know what it is a person really wants to do, achieve or own, you can in most cases plan a strategy to help that person achieve their own goals. This is where the really effective manager comes into his or her own. Sometimes the first stage may be to give the person an opportunity to be involved in some further training. Good training is highly motivating for those who are fortunate enough to receive it. In the UK, we will undervalue the importance of giving people exposure to further knowledge and skill development.

Research has shown that investing in people and giving them chances to enhance their skills are more conducive towards staff retention. It used to be believed that, by training people, companies would lose them to the competition – the opposite is in fact the case.

In other cases, it may be as simple as working out a career path. With a hobby or in the sporting world, a similar strategy is often adopted, planning a strategy for development.

Employers must accept that if they do not have the vehicle of opportunity to satisfy the goal or the ambition of the individual, that person will move on to new pastures and new career opportunities. Long gone are the days when people joined a company and stayed there for the remainder of their working lives. In some instances, headhunters, recruiters and personnel officers will actually turn people down if they have been with one company for too long a period.

It is far better to have an open style of management whereby it is accepted by the manager and the employee that at some stage the employee will be moving on. It is far healthier when the employer takes pride and personal satisfaction from seeing their ex-employees advancing successfully through their careers and achieving outstanding results. I am personally thrilled to hear the news of all my ex-employees and of the successes in their lives.

Let's list some ideas for motivating and inspiring the person:

1. Be a good listener

To have any chance at all of inspiring the person, one has to have the confidence and the respect of the individual. This must mean, therefore, that the motivator has to become, to a certain extent, a confidant. We have all heard the expression: 'A problem shared is a problem halved; a joy that is shared is a joy that is doubled.' Therefore, employees, associates and colleagues should have the knowledge that you are approachable, that they can speak to you, that they won't get bawled at, that you will always give them a fair hearing and that you will be prepared to listen to their problems and worries.

2. Be trustworthy

It follows on that if you are going to be a confidant and have the respect of others, you do not pass on what is told to you. When somebody tells you their secret, they should be totally secure and confident that it will remain as it should be – a secret. So many managers do not retain the loyalty or respect of their subordinates because they are unable to keep their mouths shut. It is no wonder that the people who are good listeners as well as having the integrity not to pass on confidences invested in them by others will always attract people into their company.

I knew a very great lady who, even into her late seventies, when she was very crippled with arthritis, was continually visited by a great mass of various friends, neighbours and family. And even more extraordinary, it appeared that at least 60 to 70 per cent of her visitors were under the age of 30 and they all seemed to leave her company with a smile on their face and a spring in their step. She listened to them, she was interested in them and then she encouraged them.

3. Catch them doing something right

There are many varied ways of raising a person's motivational level and perhaps one of the simplest of all involves utilizing that great expression: 'Catch them doing something right.' All managers will tell staff when they do something wrong, but very few managers tell their people when they do it right. Criticism sounds best when the result is criticized, not the person. So do, of course, be prepared to look for improvement, but, I must emphasize, try only to criticize the result of the action, not the action itself.

How about building up a list of other ways of raising motivational levels that you can use with your own people?

Later on in this book, under Incentive Contests (Chapter 11), we look at ways of rewarding results, but even some of the simplest forms of communication can raise levels of motivation and performance enormously. A 'thank you' letter to an employee for some task, contribution, support or quantified result will be received with pleasure and, in some cases, even treasured. A handwritten thank you letter or card is a hundred times more effective than an e-mail.

4. Show you believe in them

People will rise to the level of belief that their manager has in them. So, in order to inspire an individual to greater levels of achievement or performance, you 'the inspirator', must believe they can do it and demonstrate your belief in them with expressions like, 'I know you can do it', 'You're very good at this' or 'This is one of your strong points.' Not only must you show your belief and, of course, confidence in the individual concerned, but let this be seen and heard by their peers. Of course, you must be realistic, and not diminish your own credibility by using a 'You're good at that'-type phrase about something the individual is manifestly incompetent at. If these guidelines are followed, people will often rise to the level of achievement according to the belief that you have in them.

5. A positive message

The motivator has to motivate, so always have something encouraging to say. Make sure you are the sort of person who you would like to meet and take inspiration from.

6. Set challenges

Some people have a short fuse; others have a long fuse. Some get started on the success ladder whilst still at school and others are still on the first rung at the age of 50. I believe Colonel Sanders of Kentucky Fried Chicken fame didn't get started until he was an octogenarian!

Rupert Murdoch, the press and media baron, now in his seventies, has often been described as the most powerful man in the world and continually looks to acquire new media opportunities. As I write this book, apparently China is becoming his next major challenge.

So sometimes people have to be challenged in order to light the fuse that sparks them into activity and achievement. Such challenges can be in many varied forms, as we will see in the positive examples discussed later in this book. But they can also be negative-type challenges: 'I bet you can't' or 'I don't think you could'. Challenges must always be communicated with good will rather than bad feeling or ill will.

7. Be careful with the negative challenge

This is almost the same as point 6 above, but is said with ill humour, little goodwill and a lack of belief. The even more dangerous extension is the negative challenge that can become an insult. A management style occasionally used involves a manager ignoring an individual in their team if they are consistently under-performing. I might add that this is only carried out as a last-ditch exercise after every other form of management communication and motivation has been used. The challenge can be prefaced with: 'As you are completely useless, and I'll be wasting my time anyhow, I bet you couldn't...'

Let me emphasise once again that this is an *extremely* dangerous form of motivation and, if successful, does not build up the management/employee relationship. But, if having achieved success through this form of motivation, time will build a bond if the manager is truly a motivator.

8. Avoid sarcasm

Sarcasm is very rarely understood and is usually misinterpreted. It is certainly not a motivational style of communication if the motivator wants the other person to listen and respond to what they say. Sarcastic communicators think they are funny. They are, of course, very unfunny and sooner or later it makes people cynical. Cynicism and sarcasm can never lead to a motivational form of communication.

9. Gather the honey

On fine warm days, the worker bees go out to gather the

pollen, fill their honey sacks and return to the hive. Are you the sort of person who other people want to return to when they have achieved some success? Let me also ask, who do you want to tell when you have achieved some success? Who do you want to share that joy or pleasure with? To motivate another person, you must be the sort of person who they instantly want to tell over the telephone or by calling to see you, and your response should always be one of genuine enthusiasm, pleasure, interest and genuinely complimentary. You attract more bees with honey than you do with vinegar.

Motivating the person at work

	Yes	No
Is there a clear job description?		
Does the person know the other team members?		
Does the person know the organization?		
Have targets been agreed and quantified?		
Does the person have sufficient authority to achieve?		
Has the person been (or is the person going to be) adequately trained?		
Do they receive sufficient recognition?		
Are there emphases on results and achievement?		
Does the person see a chance to develop?		
Is their performance regularly reviewed?		
Is enough time spent listening to, developing and counselling the person?		
Are grievances dealt with promptly?		
Does the person feel their work contributes to the overall result?		

Pocket Reminders

To motivate someone successfully:

■ Remove the demotivators
■ Find out what they want
■ Show them how to get it

Now the inspiration:

■ Be a good listener
■ Be trustworthy
■ Catch them doing something right
■ Show you believe in them
■ Be a good news carrier
■ Set challenges
■ Be careful with the negative challenge
■ Avoid sarcasm
■ Attract people who achieve successes

Wise Words

When a man blames others for his failures it's a good idea to credit others with his successes.

Howard Newton

8

Motivating the Team

It's amazing what can be achieved with a highly motivated team. On leaving agricultural college, I did one year's work experience on a farm in Cranbrook in Kent. A group of us got together and formed the Cranbrook Rugby Club. There was a great deal of opposition and many problems facing us, the first being that we had no pitch on which to play; the second being no money even to buy the rugby shirts. Eventually, the pitch was loaned by a local school and slowly the rest of the difficulties were overcome. The inspiration, motivation and driving force came from two people – the McMinnies brothers – and it was their inspiration that fired the rest of the team to believe:

- that we had something to prove;
- that we were pioneering;
- that the recognition was stimulating;
- that the rewards of success were shared.

There was some lack of skill and talent in that first year but there *was* incredible enthusiasm, determination and motivation.

We trained as a team one evening a week and then rewarded our effort at the White Hart pub. That first season, we played

15 matches and didn't lose a game. Why? It certainly wasn't the skill, but it most undoubtedly was a motivated team. Unfortunately, the next year, we didn't do quite so well. A few of the original team members moved away, the McMinnies brothers were unable to devote so much time and new people joined and the original motivational causes were no longer apparent.

This is a further good lesson for all managers and motivators of teams. Remember the law: **Motivation, once established, does not last.** This is why very few sporting teams are consistently at the top. It requires great skill and strength of discipline for any team to stay continually at the top.

The difference between a team and a group is that a team is interdependent for overall performance. The *Concise Oxford Dictionary* defines team work as 'combined effort, organized co-operation'.

In the sales world, sales leaders must understand the difference between a sales team and a sales force. In some companies, it is essential to create a sales team that shares information and works collectively to achieve given criteria and sales results. Individuals should then be rewarded as a team and share in the commission and bonuses. In other sales environments, a sales force in which the individual succeeds or fails upon his or her own actions is necessary. In such an environment, individuals are rewarded for their individual performance.

In the sporting world, we acclaim teams and we praise team spirit. If only managers and supervisors in the business community applied the same principles. Understanding the principles that exist in the sporting world, it would be truly amazing to see the results that could be achieved.

Keep to your Principles

So let's now look at some of those principles that can be applied both socially and commercially and let me begin by stressing the importance of this expression: 'The climate must be right.' This is a principle that, of course, applies not only to motivating yourself, but also to turning a group into a team. In order for people to be motivated and happy in their work, there are five common sense principles to be followed.

1. They should be capable

People must be capable of carrying out the job, task or position that they are given. We have all heard the expression: 'A square peg in a round hole.' In the sales world, it is often considered essential that in order to be a sales manager one has to be a good salesperson. This is true, but it does not mean that a good salesperson will necessarily be a good sales manager. SOME-BODY WHO IS NOT A GOOD SALESPERSON CAN NEVER BE A GOOD SALES MANAGER.

While attending a regional sales meeting of one of my clients I saw a most unhappy situation. The team of salespeople was led by a sales manager who was obviously the 'square peg in the round hole'. His title should have been 'sales administration manager', which was where his skill, talents, confidence and enthusiasm really lay. The team of people were suffering as well inasmuch as the team was at the bottom of the league table of 12 regions.

The sales manager had a very introverted personality, had never really achieved any sales success and was much more comfortable with a computer than with people. He should never have been put into the position of sales manager or a leader of people.

2. They must be fit for it

Yes, people should be able, through training and through personal development programmes, to be fit for the part they have to play in their team. But let me also touch on another of the old clichés: 'You can take a horse to water, but you can't make it drink.' If the individual does not want to be trained or does not want the post that they have been given, they will never become fit for it.

3. They must not over-indulge

For people to be happy in their work, they should not do too much of it. They must get the balance right. We all know the expression: 'All work and no play makes Jack a very dull boy.' It also produces staleness in performance if people are not getting a contrast of activities in their lives. Contrast is absolutely essential in maintaining maximum enthusiasm and effectiveness.

4. They must experience success

For individuals in a team to achieve success, they must be happy and that happiness can be developed through the enjoyment of the success feeling.

Here we are again mentioning that law of success that says: **seeing ourselves progressing motivates us.**

5. They must have the right attitude

In this chapter, we must remember that we are looking at ideas that can apply equally to a team at work, at play, or engaged in any other activity.

When people are at play, following a social hobby or charitable activity, they are less likely to take offence at the four-letter word – WORK. Work is something we do not usually do without reward, and the reward for the majority of people is money. So the example of people being happy to work when at play shows that it is a person's **attitude** towards work that is so important.

If people would accept this, then in most cases, the more successful they will be at their work, the more rewards they will receive. This in turn can only mean greater enjoyment when they are away from their work at weekends, evenings and holidays.

I never cease to be amazed by the differences in people's attitude to work. In some organizations I visit, particularly in the advertising and sales promotion world, I see people starting at 7.30 in the morning and going on until 7.00 and 8.00 o'clock at night. Not, of course, every day of the week, but regularly and when necessary. And in other companies I see people doing the proverbial 9–5 and rushing out of the door at one minute to five. They can't wait to leave their place of work.

This is a classical indication of poor management, resulting in low job satisfaction and little commitment, and is a major sign that leadership is required. Don't blame the people – train the managers. Now I am not saying of course that people should work long hours, but you do not see people clock-watching in companies with good, motivated leaders.

Creating the Team Environment

The climate must be right. Here are a further 11 key tips that create the right environment for the team to become naturally self-motivated. This surely is one of the great principles of good motivational leadership, that it is not something that is imposed or forced, but is a natural positive climate for motivational expression.

1. Positive working conditions

What this means is that the equipment, tools and systems that team members are required to use do, in fact, actually work. Every one of us has experienced at some time the frustration of faulty equipment or systems. I am not saying that when something breaks down it causes demotivation; what I am saying is that if it *remains* unrepaired then, undoubtedly, demotivation sets in.

Working conditions should, of course, be clean and comfortable. People should be proud of the place in which they work – and the balance here is crucial. I am certainly no expert on optimum square feet per employee, etc, but I have seen extremely low productivity where people are put into large luxurious offices with far too much space and equally I have seen incredible productivity and motivational team spirit where people are almost on top of each other in a situation, where people are almost seizing a chair or desk the moment it is vacated.

Checklist

	Yes	No
Is the working environment positive?		
Are toilet facilities clean and cared for?		
Is the entrance inviting?		
Is the equipment repaired immediately upon breakdown?		
Is there a facility to eat and 'break out'?		
Have organizational changes caused stress?		
Are there many people on short-term contracts?		
Is there a 'them and us' division between staff and management?		
Have there been recent redundancies?		
Are rewards and salaries fair?		
Does the MD/CEO walk the floor?		
Does the MD/CEO know people's names?		

It costs very little in most cases to create a positive working environment.

2. Team players

All members of a team must be team players and it is often worthwhile making the effort to ensure this is the case by using personality profiling or psychometric testing – try contacting the RDO office for these (their Web site is supplied at the back of this book).

Sometimes, tough decisions have to be taken in replacing people who are not team players. Rest assured, others within the team will understand when they are on the receiving end of a non-team player.

3. The culture of priorities

I hope you haven't forgotten the greatest management principle in the world:

Whatever you reward, you will get more of.

For a motivated team, therefore, it is essential that all members of the team know what their individual priorities are in working towards the team's objective.

What does the manager reward or recognize? Let's look at some examples:

▥ Do people get rewarded who look busy and work long hours rather than those who get results?
▥ Are demands made for quality work, but unrealistic deadlines set?
▥ Is company loyalty demanded and talked about, but with no offer of job security?
▥ Are people given large budget increases after exhausting their resources, yet frugality demanded?
▥ Are people frightened to try something different because of fear of chastisement when what is really needed is creative input?
▥ Is teamwork demanded, yet one member of a team played off against another?

The culture of priorities is very much linked with the behaviour that is expected. People will always behave the way the reward mechanism has trained them.

4. A common goal

There must be a common goal, an objective or even a cause to fight for. It is utterly impossible to motivate a team of people without one of these three things. When creating what I am now going to call the 'common goal', at the risk of sounding obvious, remember the goal must interest the people.

It is no good imposing a goal that stimulates the manager, but does not interest the participants. This leads on to the importance of creating the goal by a collective decision-making process. This is really plain common sense, but it is staggering how many companies and organizations do not seem to adhere to this principle.

It is possible to create excellent incentive programmes or to organize and present some great motivational seminars. Or you could go to the other extreme of motivation – which is to threaten people with the sack. But that can never be as successful as getting people involved and genuinely participating.

Goals that people have some responsibility for setting are much more likely to be achieved than those that are imposed. And common goals do become effective motivators. In creating a common goal, the motivator must also create the stimulation of new goals from time to time. Cast your mind back to the example I gave earlier in this chapter of the Cranbrook Rugby Club, where through certain circumstances, the original motivational causes were no longer apparent.

5. Have a vision

Mission statements were a must, and were no doubt dreamt up by some management consultant. They have now proved to be completely ineffectual. Mission statements were of course created with the belief that it would be of benefit for the staff and for their customers. Most organizations attempted to get their employees to help develop the company's mission. Eventually these wordy, virtuous statements were produced and framed in the entrance lobby. Hardly anybody could actually recall what the statement was. It was one of these appalling fads that were absolutely useless but nevertheless took up hours of creative time. Thank goodness they are now relegated to the paper shredder.

The worst mission statement I ever heard was by a company chairman in front of his 500-odd employees – the company's mission was 'to be the most profitable in their market sector'. This one was certainly dreamt up by the directors and, in this case, as of course you can quite rightly imagine, not only demotivated the employees, but lost them customers as well.

Now having a vision is very different. Not necessarily something that has to be written up and emblazoned on the walls – but a vision that allows all employees to see where their company could be. Shared equally and passionately, and enthusiastically embraced. Yes, do have a vision.

6. Maintain a high energy level

People are naturally more motivated when they are busy. They very rarely suffer from body fatigue, but they do suffer, as we have already discussed, from mental fatigue – stress. However, working really hard while avoiding stress is almost unheard of as a cause of medical complaint.

7. Remember the individual

Significance of the individual is still important, even though people are part of a team.

A team is a number of individuals who are interdependent on their overall performance, but who are still individuals in their own right. They must *individually* feel that their treatment is fair and just. They must *individually* feel that they are recognised for their contribution. They must *individually* feel that the part they play contributes towards the goal or the achievement. They must *individually* have the loyalty and respect of the manager and their colleagues.

While on the subject of loyalty and respect, let's be realistic: this is something that is earnt in life and should never be demanded or expected.

8. Team identity

Have you noticed how people are so willing to wear sweatshirts and T-shirts that are emblazoned with the name of their sporting team? It is one of the principles of motivation that we talked about earlier: group belonging motivates. So as a manager, look at every possibility of creating your team's identity.

9. Share success

Team members must be able to share in the rewards of success. You will undoubtedly have noticed at the football World Cup Final how the captain of the team is presented with the cup, which is duly kissed and held aloft, but is then passed to every member of the team, and how all team members get their own winner's medal, not just the captain or the manager.

A great example of this message was shown by Richard Branson of Virgin Airways. If you recall, early in 1993, British Airways admitted to some unethical practices and unfair acts of competition. An out-of-court settlement was agreed and some £500,000 was settled on, as well as a sum in excess of £2,000,000 to cover the costs of the legal action that was impending.

Richard Branson shared the settlement money with all the members of his staff as, from what I understand, he considered that they had been slighted as well as his company and his profits.

10. The positive team

How do the team members communicate with each other? Is it positive or is it negative? Where it is practical, team bonding can be created by the team experiencing activities outside the daily routine of work. Activity weekends, attending courses as a group and team competitions are all very worthwhile. When there is a situation created in which individuals can care for and support each other, it can contribute to a more motivated unit. If it is negative, the one absolute certainty is that the team will become an unproductive team.

It is very much the responsibility of the manager or leader to prevent negative communication spreading infectiously.

Most effective managers teach and train people on the subject of the positive and the negative. We are all aware of the expression: 'The bad apple in the barrel can pollute all the others.' And so it is with a team of people. It only takes one person to become truly negative for the remainder of that team to gradually become negative as well. And a negative team is most certainly not a motivated team.

My company, The Richard Denny Group, produces an excellent training video programme for managers on how to turn a negative person or team into a positive team. Please e-mail or write to the address given on page 157 if you would like further information.

We will be looking at this issue again in Chapter 12, Motivational Communication.

11. Motivational leadership

This heading could equally be placed at number 1 rather than here in our list of 11. The leadership style of the manager must be a *motivational* one and in Chapter 9 we cover this in detail.

If effectively managed, the above 11 key pointers to creating a motivational climate into which people can blend and function can remove the excuses – some of which may be justified – as to why people cannot be properly motivated.

Let's now look at one or two more ideas that can help towards creating a motivated team.

Take a Break Together

It is so worthwhile for employees to go away as a group. No doubt you have experienced this at some stage when you have been on a course with others. It is common that they are complete strangers prior to the course, but at the end of it, isn't it amazing how you all become more drawn together!

So by taking your team away either for training, discussion or even for a leisure trip, you will draw them closer together.

These occasions do not have to be expensive if the budgets are tight. In its simplest form, the trip can be a skittles match one evening after work or a visit to a restaurant or theatre. Then there are the more glamorous three- or four-day outward-bound-type courses.

However, a word of warning here for all managers and leaders. The clichéd expression 'Familiarity breeds contempt' is unfortunately all too accurate. So as a manager you must always be prepared to keep a certain amount of distance between yourself and your team.

Once employees or team members see or experience your own weaknesses, you will most certainly lose some of their respect. We all have our own weaknesses. It is essential, therefore, that, with the enormous responsibility any leader or manager carries, while with their team they are always on duty – or as they say in the military, 'on parade'.

To conclude this chapter, let's go back and revisit that great management principle:

You will get more of what you reward.

Pocket Reminders

To create a motivated team you must:

▓ Give the team good working conditions
▓ Explain the company's mission
▓ Give the team a goal
▓ Remember the individual members of the team
▓ Promote the individual members of the team
▓ Share success
▓ Ensure the team is positive
▓ Be a motivational leader

Wise Words

TEAMWORK
There were four people named
EVERYBODY, SOMEBODY, ANYBODY and NOBODY.
There was an important job to be done
and EVERYBODY was asked to do it.
EVERYBODY was sure SOMEBODY would do it.
ANYBODY could have done it,
but NOBODY did it.
SOMEBODY got angry about that,
because it was EVERYBODY's job.
EVERYBODY thought ANYBODY could do it but
NOBODY realised that EVERYBODY wouldn't do it.
It ended up that EVERYBODY blamed SOMEBODY
when NOBODY did what ANYBODY could have done.

9

Motivational Leadership

A great military general, when speaking to his officers, stated: 'See that your men have reason to respect you.'

As I have already said, respect is earned and can never, and should never, be demanded. We all judge leaders more by what they do than by what they say. In commerce, industry and business, managers who supervise others are, of course, salespeople. They have to sell their ideas and work practices. They have to sell good ideas and good work habits. Successful managers appreciate the power of setting a good example.

They realize that they are being watched as they go about their day-to-day tasks and that their own example will carry much greater influence and, of course, produce better results than verbal advice, lecturing or any other communication.

Sadly, some managers feel that when they have reached a certain level they are no longer subject to the same standards that they expect from their subordinates. They almost believe that it is their job to tell other people what to do, regardless of whether or not they do it themselves. The great tragedy is that, if they don't believe in something strongly enough to practise it themselves, then telling others to do it does really very little good.

We all know that the strengths and weaknesses in any

department or organization can often mirror those of the people who run it. If you, as a manager, have difficulty getting the people who work for you to measure up to the standards upon which you insist, how about firstly taking a look at yourself. Do you measure up to these standards? Are you practising what you preach?

The 10 Principles of Leadership

So let's now list the 10 principles of motivational leadership.

1. Set goals

Set a realistic goal and *go for it*. People are inspired when they work for a manager with a purpose. As we discussed under 'goal setting', goals must be achievable, but as a management style it can be very motivating when managers set higher goals. There is always the risk that you might not achieve them. This doesn't really matter, however, as long as it's not a case of continual failure, as this will cause loss of credibility and will affect people's belief that they can achieve future goals.

2. Set an example

Recognize that, over a period of time, subordinates tend to become carbon copies of their chief. People do look to their superiors for guidance. You will see in so many different organizations how this emulating, either consciously or subconsciously, not only filters through to work practices, but also to style of clothes and appearance, the way people communicate with each other, their time keeping, their convictions and maybe even the newspapers they read. The list is endless.

So once again, what sort of people do you want to have working for you? Or if you are a leader outside the world of business, maybe in the sporting world or in the teaching profession, what sort of results – be they behavioural or communicative – are you hoping for? Remember, it starts with you!

3. Constantly improve

Be a progressive thinker. Employ the 'how can I do it better?' thought process. Eliminate from your thoughts and your vocabulary 'I am doing my best' and never allow the people who you are leading to think that they are doing their best. As we all know – if we want to face the truth – **we can all do better**.

In being a progressive thinker, one naturally has a thought process that always looks to the future rather than the past. And when undergoing self-analysis ask yourself this question: 'Am I worth more today than I was yesterday or last week, last month or even last year?' For a practising progressive thinker, every day is an opportunity for new experience, to gain new knowledge with the single purpose of being **a better person** at the end of the day.

4. Give yourself time to think

Spend some time in uninterrupted thought. It's really quite extraordinary and perhaps rather sad that so many leaders just do not allow themselves thinking time, and of those that do, it is not so much *allowing* themselves as snatching it, often while travelling. As we know, we have been given this incredible asset of a brain with limitless capacity, but at the same time we often inhibit its enormous power.

Put aside perhaps half an hour a day purely for thinking, and you will be staggered by the results. I personally have found that some of my most productive days have been when I have spent some time on my own in a hotel or well away from the office, other people and the telephone. You will find that your own motivational level will increase after a period of uninterrupted thinking time.

Give yourself time for a good thinking session and worries

can be put into perspective, goals and plans organized, and problems solved. Always provide yourself with a pad of blank paper and a pen to jot down your thoughts and decisions as they come tumbling out.

5. Lead without pushing

The most effective leadership is by example and not by edict. The motivated leader will lead, but not necessarily push, show but not necessarily tell.

> There is a story of General Eisenhower who, in explaining this principle to his officers, used to lay a piece of string on the floor and demonstrate that by pushing he got nowhere with the string, but by pulling, the string would follow him anywhere he wished to go.

In most team sports, the captain is normally one of the best players. But one has to accept that the best performer will not necessarily have leadership skills, although this is the norm and a prerequisite for captaincy. There are very few exceptions: Mike Brearley, the ex-English cricket captain, most certainly was one and he is held in very high esteem as being one of the greatest captains of all time. However, he accepted that he was not one of the best cricketers in terms of batting or bowling. Martin Johnson, on the other hand, the ex-England rugby captain, World Cup winner, Lions captain etc, proves the point. The calibre of that man is, of course, rare, but nevertheless an example for many business leaders to aspire to.

Continually ask yourself one question: ARE YOU LEADING BY EXAMPLE?

6. Judge by results

Expect always to be judged by results, as you, the motivated manager and leader, will judge others by results. If you were setting your own standards for a motivational leadership style, would it be one that is results orientated, following the principles that we have already discussed? Or have you created your own judging-by-results culture?

7. Build confidence

Develop a supreme confidence in yourself and your ability. This supreme confidence will inspire others and this is the motivational leadership style that can be so effective: raising other people's performance to levels they never believed they were capable of.

The 'how to's' of building confidence have already been discussed and we know that, when tackling something new, confidence may be low. But just the sheer understanding of this will help to build and retain the confidence – and at the same time will not reduce ability.

Ability is something that we acquire as a result of a strong desire.

8. Expect criticism

It's regrettable to say, but nonetheless true, that as a person becomes increasingly successful it is only a matter of time before they are criticized. One of the great British characteristics is that we search desperately for a hero, be it from the world of sport, business or politics. However, as soon as we put them onto a pedestal, with a hero's halo above them, the media has to find ways of bringing them back down again.

So if you are going to be a good leader, you should be putting your head above the parapet and making yourself vulnerable to criticism, which nearly always emanates from that most harmful and evil of all human feelings – jealousy!

9. Think of the future

Plan on doing something different tomorrow. If every day you can do something slightly different from what you did yesterday, each time doing a little bit better, you will create an inspirational leadership style that is very motivational. **The person who is always looking for something new to do every day has to have a wonderfully progressive mind.**

10. Think like a winner

This is such a good thought process to adopt. When you are confronted with a situation, be it positive or negative, try to imagine how the most successful person that you know would think and then act in the situation. If it is a sporting situation, think of the most successful player in that sport – how would they think and act? If it is a business situation, and let me use an example from the sales world, how would the most successful salesperson think and act?

10 DIFFERENCES BETWEEN A WINNER AND A LOSER

1. **A winner makes mistakes and says: 'I was wrong.'** A loser says: 'It wasn't my fault.'

2. **A winner credits his good luck for winning, even though it wasn't luck.** A loser credits his bad luck for losing, even though it wasn't luck.

3. **A winner works harder than a loser and has more time.** A loser is always 'too busy': too busy staying a failure.

4. **A winner goes through a problem.** A loser goes around it.

5. **A winner shows he's sorry by making up for it.** A loser says he's sorry but he does the same thing next time.

6. **A winner knows what to fight for and what to compromise on.** A loser compromises on what he should not and fights for what isn't worth fighting for. Every day is a battle in life, and it is very important that we are fighting for the right things and not wasting our time with trivial matters.

7. **A winner says: 'I'm good, but not as good as I ought to be.'** A loser says: 'Well, I'm not as bad as a lot of people.' A winner looks up to where he is going. A loser looks down at those who've not yet achieved the position he has.

8. **A winner respects those who are superior to him and tries to learn from them.** A loser resents those who are superior to him and tries to find fault.

9. **A winner is responsible for more than his job.** A loser says: 'I only work here.'

10. **A winner says: 'There ought to be a better way of doing it.'** A loser says: 'Why change it? That's the way it's always been done.'

The 12 Major Causes of Failure in Leadership

Although it is extremely important to know what to do when leading people, it must be just as important to know what *not* to do.

1. Inability to organize detail

Whenever a manager admits publicly or to themselves that they are too busy to give sufficient attention to any aspect of their work, they are admitting their inability to do their job effectively.

2. Unwillingness to do what they would ask another to do

When occasion demands, and let me stress this is only when the occasion *demands*, the effective manager is always willing to perform the task that he or she would ask another person to do.

It does not matter that the manager may not be able to do it as well as another – if they are unwilling to try, it can be a cause of failure.

3. Expectation of pay for what they know instead of what they do

The world does not pay people for what they know, it pays them for what they do or, perhaps more importantly, what they motivate others to do.

It is all very well having the most brilliant education, passing all the exams and degrees with a brain stacked full of knowledge. But you must remember that this is not what you are paid for. People get paid for what they **do** rather than what they **know**.

4. Fear of competition from others

Whatever we fear invariably happens. The manager who fears that one of his followers could take his position is almost sure to realize that fear sooner or later.

So many managers are afraid that their own position is threatened that they try to hold back people below them rather than build them up in order to protect themselves. We have all heard the expression: 'You can't hold good people down.'

5. Lack of creative thinking

Without creative thinking, the manager is incapable of creating plans and setting goals with which to guide staff effectively. It can also be described as **lateral thinking.**

The blinkered manager will miss opportunities and will not inspire his people.

6. The 'I' syndrome

The manager who claims all the credit for achievements of his or her team is certain to be met with resentment. The completely effective leader will claim none of the credit, but will ensure that, when there is any, it goes to the team.

7. Over-indulgence

In whatever form, over-indulgence may manifest itself, not only will it destroy the endurance and the vitality of the manager, but it will also cause a loss of respect from the team. Over-indulgence can be manifested in many and varied forms – from alcohol abuse to womanizing!

8. Disloyalty

The manager who is not loyal to his colleagues, both above him and below him, will not maintain his leadership for very long.

A lack of loyalty is one of the major causes of failure and loss of respect in every walk of life.

> Loyalty is like respect – it is earned and can never be demanded.

9. Emphasis on the 'authority of leadership'

An example of this is: 'Do this or you're fired!' Successful leaders lead by encouraging and not by trying to instil fear in their followers. Instilling fear falls within the category of leadership by force. History has shown that this is an effective form of leadership. It does work – *but it never lasts!*

A manager who uses fear as a tool of motivation will find it effective the first and possibly the second time it is used. But then the power starts to diminish. It is then only a matter of time before authority is destroyed.

10. Emphasis of title

Some managers make a great play of their title and have it displayed on their office door. Usually, the manager who makes too much of his title has little else to make very much of.

11. A lack of understanding of the destructive effects of a negative environment

It is utterly impossible to be a great leader or a motivational manager without a deep understanding of the extreme harm caused by a negative environment. We will discuss in more detail the prevention and the cure of such an environment under the heading of Motivational Communication in Chapter 12.

12. A lack of common sense

Perhaps one way of illustrating this list of the 12 major causes of failure in leadership is the manager who becomes so heavenly minded and ultra positive he is no earthly good.

There was a story of a young manager who felt the one thing that was lacking in his life was positive thinking. So in his determination to rectify this, he booked himself into a three-week positive thinking course in the United States, and for three solid weeks he was totally brainwashed by the power of positive thinking.

After returning to his company, he told everybody that what was missing from their lives was the power of positive thinking – that once you have it, absolutely everything becomes possible.

As the days went by, his colleagues became more and more cynical and then, in total desperation to prove to his cynical colleagues the power of positive thinking, he said: 'I am going to the top of our office building and I am going to jump off and I am not going to hit the ground!'

His friends and colleagues thought: 'This is great – we've really got to see this!' So they all trooped to the top of the building and heard that no earthly good manager announce again: 'I will demonstrate the power of positive thinking. I am going to leap off and I will not hit the ground!'

And he jumped.

Going past the fifth storey he was overhead to say: 'So far, so good...'

So one must remember, with all human characteristics, the EXTREMES ARE DANGEROUS.

The 12 Major Attributes of Leadership

1. A willingness to try the untried

No employee wishes to be led by a manager who lacks courage and self-confidence. It is a positive leadership style that takes on challenging tasks or takes opportunities that have not been tried before.

A successful sales manager will go out and sell when the marketplace is really tough or when the salespeople are under extreme pressure. That manager knows that he or she risks being unsuccessful, but nevertheless, by leading by example, will maintain the motivation of the team.

2. Self-motivation

The manager who cannot motivate himself has not got the slightest chance of being able to motivate others.

3. A keen sense of what is fair

This is a great quality of an effective leader. In order to retain the respect of the team, a manager must be sensitive to what is fair and just. The leadership style whereby all people are treated justly and equally always creates a feeling of security. I have found this many times to be extremely constructive and a great leveller.

4. Definite plans

The motivated leader always has goals and has planned their achievement. He or she plans the work and then works the plan.

5. Decision 'stickability'

The manager who wavers in the decision-making process shows that he is unsure of himself, whereas an effective leader makes a decision after having given sufficient thought to the problem. He even considers the possibility that the decision being taken may turn out to be the wrong one.

Most people who make decisions will get some of them wrong. However, this does not necessarily diminish respect from their followers. Let's be realistic: a manager may make more decisions that are wrong than the followers make that are right, but an effective leader makes the decision and shows his conviction and belief in that decision by sticking to it.

The followers then have the strength to fight for that decision as well.

6. The habit of doing more than one is paid for

One of the penalties of leadership is a willingness to do more than is required of one's followers. The manager who arrives before the employees and leaves a little bit later is one example of this attribute of leadership.

7. A positive personality

Followers respect this quality. It not only inspires confidence, but also builds and maintains an enthusiastic team.

8. Empathy

The successful leader must have the ability to put himself in the shoes of his followers – to be able to see the world from their side. He does not have to agree with it but must be able to see how they feel and understanding their viewpoint.

9. Mastery of detail

The successful leader understands and carries out every detail of his or her job and, of course, has the knowledge and the skill to master the responsibilities that go with the position.

Henry Ford took a journalist to court for libel, as the journalist had claimed in an article that Henry Ford was not only a bit dull but really rather stupid.

The defending barrister at the libel action put Henry Ford into the witness box and bombarded him with questions on general knowledge and history, asking questions such as: 'Will you explain Einstein's theory of relativity?'

To the majority of the questions Henry Ford replied with: 'I am sorry, I don't know the answer to that.'
The lawyer turned to the jury after this lengthy questioning and said: 'I think I've proved my point.'
To which Henry Ford then replied: 'Hang on a minute. You have been asking me all these questions for the past two hours, none of which, if I knew the answers, could help me to run my business or help me to build more effective motor cars. On my desk I have a console of buttons and if I needed to get the answer to one of those questions while in my office I know exactly which button to press and could provide you with the answer within seconds.'
He went on to win his case.

10. Willingness to assume full responsibility

Another penalty of leadership is the accepted practice of taking responsibility for the mistakes of followers. Should a follower make a mistake, perhaps through incompetence, the leader must consider that it is himself who has failed. If the leader tries to shift this responsibility, he will not remain the leader.

The effective leader accepts the cliché: 'The buck stops here.'

11. Duplication

The successful leader is always looking for ways of duplicating skills in other people. In this way, he develops others and is effectively able to be in many different places at the same time.

Perhaps this, of all the necessary attributes, has to be the greatest for leaders – the ability to develop other leaders is vital. One can always judge a leader by the number of people in whom they have duplicated their talents, and those who they have developed and brought into the world as great leaders.

Andrew Carnegie, one of the greatest motivators and leaders the world has ever known, created 32 millionaires out of his organization.

12. A deep belief in their principles

I personally love the expression: 'Unless we stand for something, we will fall for anything.'

Nothing worth achieving is ever very easy. The successful leader has a determination to achieve goals, no matter what obstacles come along, and believes in what he or she is doing with a determination to fight for it.

Wise Words

There is no safe way to be a good leader. You do not win all the time and you have to learn that failure is part of the leadership game – so long as you don't make the same mistake twice.

Sir Colin Marshall

10

Incentive Motivation

It is quite extraordinary how the majority of people find a balance in their employer–employee relationship during their working lives. Many people work just hard enough so they don't get fired and in return their employer pays them just enough so that they don't leave. It is on this sort of happy or unhappy basis that life proceeds. I often wonder how many people really love their work and how many employers really enjoy the company of the people they have working for them.

But, as we have discussed already, when the happiness and enjoyment factor is high on both sides, success is inevitable.

A successful incentive programme will not only increase profits, but can also inspire staff loyalty and raise morale. Most people seem to go to work to do a reasonable job, but not an exceptional one.

Yet these same people will devote many hours to hobbies and charities without any monetary reward and do an exceptional job. What they do get, however, is **recognition**.

We have all got friends or colleagues who devote enormous amounts of energy and time to organizations such as the Round Table or Rotary. We also have friends who have a greater interest in their extra-curricular activities than they have in their work.

I have one good friend with whom I was at school and we met up again a while ago. His great interest and love was Freemasonry, to the point where nearly all his free time was devoted to that occupation. In his case, it was very much because of the recognition he received in this activity, which he certainly wasn't getting at work. Unfortunately, the sad point is that it eventually destroyed his marriage.

As with everything else, over-indulgence can become destructive. The **recognition** can almost become like a drug.

If such people were to apply the same effort to their work practice, untold rewards could be reaped.

A few years ago, I was listening to a great motivational speaker – Mr Peter Riggs. He stated what he considered to be the three greatest rewards of the universe:

1. To do the thing you enjoy doing for the sheer pleasure of doing it or, in other words, to be truly happy and content at one's work. This of course is the difference between the pain and pleasure. We will naturally avoid actions or activity that may cause pain and are drawn to those that will give us pleasure. Sadly, to take a negative example here, people will often opt for the short-term pleasure but will suffer the long-term pain – this of course is the abuse of alcohol and drugs.
2. Recognition – in all its various forms.
3. Money – and money only becomes a prime motivator if there is not a sufficient amount of it coming in to meet one's immediate daily requirements (paying the rent or the mortgage, providing food for the table and paying for the essentials, such as electricity, gas, telephone, etc).

Many managers make the mistake of thinking that money is the prime motivational requirement. Yet these same managers may be promoted to positions with monetary reward packages lower than those of some of their employees.

The majority of trained managers will have heard of Maslow's hierarchy of needs. I don't propose to discuss this in any detail here, but what I do want to emphasize is that people's aspirations, requirements and demands obviously change throughout their lives.

In this chapter, you will see how you can achieve greater performance. This should lead to better results through, firstly, understanding the power of an incentive or motivational programme and then through learning how to organize and promote such a programme.

Recognition

Let us now concentrate our thoughts on the importance of recognition and what it really means.

My own belief is that it is the most powerful incentive for motivation. In it simplest form, recognition can be a simple 'thank you'. This, of course, is best and most effectively given in public, where other workmates or colleagues can hear that gratitude being expressed.

We all know the extraordinary lengths people will go to in order to gain some recognition. How people love to appear on TV, on the radio, to have their photograph in the local paper. In the United Kingdom there is still incredible interest and prestige in the Honours List. Nearly every profession has some method of recognizing its outstanding performers – the most obvious are the Oscar nominations and the Emmy awards. Almost every profession or business organization has some national award scheme: from advertising to motor cars; from corsetry manufacturing to black-pudding making.

For some years, Jack Thornley of Thornley's of Chorley in Lancashire was the European Champion Black Pudding Maker. Tremendous prestige was earned from this recognized award! In the armed services, medals are awarded. In the sporting world, the winner is placed on the highest platform.

So, accepting the power of recognition, let's now go through a few examples that can be used in the business world. For those of you who are commercially minded, you will be pleased to hear it is the cheapest and most cost effective of all forms of incentive.

Cost-effective incentives

Sales mangers should circulate lists showing the sales results of each individual in their sales team. In very large sales organizations this can be broken down into league tables and when these tables are published, every individual will look for their own name first. Inevitably, the only people who are likely to object to this will be those at the bottom of the list or league.

Certificates of achievement can be awarded, and these are best presented already framed. These certificates do get hung. They also act as an ongoing reminder of achievement. They act as a spur when people see them on the wall and think 'I want one of those'. It is well worthwhile making sure that the certificates are on good-quality parchment-type paper, are well designed and professionally printed.

Always ask yourself the testing question: 'Would I be proud to receive and hang one of my certificates?'

In all business and commerce operations, people can be motivated by a change of job title. This is sometimes the only way of preventing the loss of an otherwise high-performing individual. Think up a new or more prestigious title.

For example, these are some of the titles that people have changed themselves:

- Groom has been changed to equine technician.
- A rat catcher to a pest control officer.
- A traveller to a sales executive.
- A housewife to a home executive.

If you can't think what to call somebody, and you really don't know what they do, how about Vice President?!

Wall plaques can be presented as well as the traditional cups and trophies. No doubt you will have seen in some organizations that people are given recognition through the tie that they wear; in others, it is in the car that they drive. In yet another, which I consider more dangerous, people are given named parking places for their vehicles. Dangerous because this really can become extremely divisive. I have seen companies where staff, as they move up the hierarchy, are given different places to eat in the canteen or even different parts in the company dining room. In some businesses, some people are allowed to enter and leave by a different door and, yet again, in other companies, people's status is judged by the size of the budget they are responsible for.

All of these examples are getting the principles of recognition dangerously wrong. Firstly, because they divide, and secondly because **you get more of what you reward**. In business, success does not come from how much you *spend*, but how much you *earn*.

Recognition can also be given if one has an in-house magazine, newsletter or some other publication, in which, wherever possible, a photograph of the high-performing individual should be included. People will always look at the photographs first.

The most effective managers and leaders will always give the recognition and make the presentations in public, but will follow this up with a personal congratulatory letter. As we all know, these letters never end up in a waste-paper basket.

Early in my career, although working for myself, I was being controlled by a very effective sales manager, Barry Wells. At that time I was working in a multi-level organization marketing household products. One of the recognition schemes in operation was known as the Diamond Pin Award Scheme. Basically, it boiled down to the fact that the more people sold, the more or the bigger the diamonds they got in a lapel pin — and I might add that these very attractive diamond pins were awarded both to husband and wife or to both partners, even though only one may have been actively involved. At the end of an incredibly busy three months where I was away from home a great deal of the time, I had achieved enough volume to win the highest of these awards.

I was some 200 miles from my home staying in a hotel in Plymouth. On phoning home, my wife informed me that she had received the largest bouquet of flowers that anybody had ever seen with a note attached to it that said, 'Thank you for all your support', signed Barry Wells.

As you can imagine, the very small cost of that action reaped countless rewards as the months went by.

The second point I want to make in relating this personal story is that, wherever possible, give recognition to both partners, even though it may only be one who is the actual achiever.

Try to remember names

Let's now change our thinking for a minute or two towards other forms that recognition can take. The sweetest sound in the English language is the sound of your own name. The most senior executive who, while on the shop floor, knows the names of all his employees, and perhaps even their partners' names and some other personal details, will be held in great reverence by the workforce.

Not all of us are gifted with brilliant memories, but a little bit of planning and preparation and maybe even briefing by junior managers can overcome a lapse in memory. Remembering people's birthdays and anniversaries is another great form of recognition.

And finally, before we leave this section, how about putting up in your own reception area the photograph and the name of the highest achiever in the top categories each month?

Money

Let us now move on to the third great reward: money.

Money, as we have already said, is not an incentive unless a person has an insufficient amount coming in for his or her immediate requirements. Therefore, if money is to be used as an incentive, it has to be of considerable quantity. You can provide as an award or a prize a plaque or a cup that may only cost £10 or £15, or a piece of cut-glass crystal that has been engraved. But try motivating an individual on a salary in excess of £20,000 with a £10 or £15 cash prize!

Another trouble with using money as an incentive is that it can be spent on household bills, which will leave no lasting advancement for the individual. Money has to be of a considerable sum to be an effective incentive and motivator, and the quantity that is on offer must, of course, relate to the salary package of the individual. Somebody on a £20,000 per annum salary could undoubtedly be motivated by a £1,000 incentive.

Now let's get this into perspective. I am not saying here that money does not work. If it is part of a commission structure, salary package, bonus or company performance shareout it can be successful. More and more companies are showing, by getting people involved with share ownership and an interest in the overall profitability of their company, the successes that can be achieved.

The interesting thing is that most people believe that money is the biggest incentive, which it is not. Isn't it interesting how people spend money in an attempt to get recognition?

Charitable giving is a great example of this point. It is extremely important for charitable collections to give maximum recognition and 'thank you's' to people for their contributions to charitable work. Very few major donations are given anonymously. People will spend a great deal of money buying tickets to get into the Royal Enclosure at Ascot. The facilities of the Royal Enclosure are certainly not what is being bought – it is the prestige of being seen there.

During the 1980s and 1990s, credit cards were almost a status symbol, and the card companies were forever thinking up more creative ways not only to get people to pay for the card subscription, but also to spend more. So Gold Cards were created, followed by Platinum, followed by Super Platinum and so on. But as with so many status symbols, not only is there a price to pay, but they lose their glamour as people become more aware and more logical. Nevertheless, there will always be new status symbols. As I write this book, holidays and/or second homes can almost be classified as status symbols.

Pocket Reminders

The three greatest incentives are:

- ▪ Happiness
- ▪ Recognition
- ▪ Money

Never forget them!

Wise Words

Supreme common sense is worth a great deal more than intellect. Effective managers have a great deal of common sense, allied with a lot of drive.

Sir Michael Edwardes

11

Incentive Contests

Let us now have a look at the rules and principles of setting up an incentive programme within an organization. I am going to call this, for the sake of simplicity, a contest.

Let me first of all establish a concept – all contests that are organized and run successfully are self-financing and do not become a cost. They are paid for not by those who win but by those who do not win, and have raised their level of performance in attempting to win. Such people will also spur others to greater levels of achievement.

The Five Golden Rules

Break these five basic rules and your contest will almost certainly not be a success. Many of you reading this section of the book will approach a contest or an incentive programme with some scepticism, either because you have been on the receiving end of one that demotivated you or because you have put one into practice that was a complete flop. Sadly, many do fail because they break these rules. If you have had experience of failure, please re-analyse it from the information in this chapter and then try again.

1. Contests that work are those in which everyone has a chance to win. If they do not have that chance, they will not

even try. This is the first reason why a contest might not work.

The second reason is even more dangerous: the contest can work from the point of view of getting people striving for a goal, but after its completion it might destroy future attitudes towards contests. This can be shown using the example of a raffle-type contest in the sales world, where each sale that takes place qualifies the salesperson for a raffle ticket. The theory is that the more sales made, the more chances of winning a prize. At the end of the qualifying period, the raffle is drawn and it *can* happen that one of the lowest-performing salespeople wins first prize because, as we all know, a raffle is chance, not luck. This can cause massive demotivation in those who have really striven to achieve.

2. Long-term contests are of little value if one is attempting to increase business immediately. This is not to say that long-term contests are of no value – they are. Many organizations have their annual awards: salesperson of the year, manager of the year, etc. They are incredibly important and should always be in existence.

   But if one wants an immediate uplift or an instant change of results, the maximum time the contest should run is three months. For those of you who have run longer-term contests, no doubt you will have found that you achieved the increased performance in the month before the contest was due to close. So it is therefore advisable that if you organize a long-term contest, you have a secondary shorter-term contest running alongside it.

   Having said that, you should ideally only have one contest running at any one time. The long-term or secondary contests do not attract the continual attention or publicity that the short-term contest does. Never have two short-term contests running concurrently. It is the old sales principle – you can only ever sell one product at a time.

3. Whenever you are constructing a contest, ask yourself: 'What do we want to achieve with this?' This may sound

like common sense, but it is quite amazing how few people do ask themselves this question. Let me remind you once again of the greatest management principle in the world – **you will get more of what you reward.**

4. Prizes, as we have already said, should not be in money but in some tangible form. The prizes that one can give can range from the engraved crystal glass through to the Christmas hamper; bottles of wine to a selection from a pre-prepared catalogue of gifts. There are many excellent companies that will put together a superb catalogue of prizes or gifts. Some of these do, of course, relate to a points structure very similar to the ones we have all experienced, from the advent of supermarket reward card schemes through to Air Miles.

The finest and most effective of all prizes is travel and time off. From weekends away to visits to exotic places around the world. But if you are ever going to use travel or holidays as an incentive, there should always be a pair of tickets. This will maximize its effect, gain fuller support and mean greater effort towards increased performance. What is wrong with a culture (providing it has no impact on others) in which, when people have finished and completed all their allocated or expected work, they can go home? We still retain the culture of paying people for the hours, not for what they do within those hours. But even if you can't change this culture, you can give people a half-day or a day off when they have achieved something beyond your expectations.

You can imagine the demotivation it could cause at home if, for example, a weekend in Amsterdam or a two-week holiday in the Seychelles were available for only one person! The incentive of a pair of tickets, however, would draw that family or partnership together – one encouraging the other, both sharing the reward.

5. Contests must set the following three questions, and unless they are readily and easily answered, your contest will be unworkable:

- Exactly what do I have to do?
- Exactly what do I get?
- By when?

Managing the Incentive Scheme

Having constructed your incentive programme or contest based solidly around the above rules, the following stages must be observed to maximize its eventual success. I want to mention again something that I referred to earlier: all contests should be totally cost effective and paid for by enhanced profits made from the increase in performance.

But contests must be sold to the participants, so the motivated manager should follow the structure below in announcing the programme to the participants.

Stage 1
Tell them what the prize(s) are. Have pictures or samples available and follow this up by giving every participant either a brochure or a photograph of the prizes.

Stage 2
Now tell them what they have to do in order to achieve these prizes and again make sure that this is fair, that everybody has a chance to participate and that they are also given clear and precise details.

Stage 3
Tell them when the contest starts and when it finishes. Again, be realistic here. Never announce your contest too early, as your high achievers or most ambitious people will hold back business until the qualifying start of the contest.

Stage 4
Finally, sell it and sell it again. This is where another mistake often occurs when people run incentive programmes. They

spend a lot of effort putting it all together, maybe even having a grand conference to launch it, and then it is very rarely talked about or promoted until its conclusion when the results are announced. You must continually publicize and talk about your programme.

Incentives do work, but please give your incentive programme the maximum chance of success by continual promotion, by constantly letting the participants know how far they are from the various prizes or stages on offer. And if you are the manager running the contest, continually talk about it to your people. Each time you speak to the people who are involved in the contest, mention it, sell it and tell them how they are doing. This can be done through face-to-face meetings or on the telephone. Send out regular written information so that people can see how close they are from winning.

> THE GREATER THE PUBLICITY, THE GREATER
> THE SUCCESS.

Success or Failure

Let me now give you an example of a contest where people can successfully compete with each other even though they are working on the proverbial 'unlevel playing field'. This is again based upon sales achievement, but the principles can, of course, be applied to other tasks and activities.

In this simple example, we have six people: Robin, Mary, Tom, Jane, Henry and Bill. They work in different parts of the country – some in very well-established territories with a known volume of business, others have just got started and others are in territories that are currently being developed.

The sales manager gets together privately with each one and agrees a target for the three-month period. See the table opposite.

	Agreed target
Robin	60
Mary	70
Tom	30
Jane	40
Henry	60
Bill	80

The prizes to be awarded are as follows:

▩ First prize to the person who achieves the greatest overall number of sales.

▩ A prize for each person who achieves exactly what they have agreed to do.

▩ A prize equal to the first prize for the person who gets the greatest percentage above their target.

Now let's see how those same people have performed by the end of the contest period.

Looking at our winners, we see that Mary got the top prize for selling the most, but Henry got the other top prize for having the greatest percentage increase. We see that Tom, who might otherwise have never been able to win a prize, was awarded his because he did exactly what he said he would do.

	Agreed target	Sales results
Robin	60	58
Mary	70	70
Tom	30	30
Jane	40	38
Henry	60	68
Bill	80	69

This is an example, in its simplest form, of a contest where everybody has a chance to win.

Let me finish this chapter with an incentive story that shows how you must be careful with what you recognize, as you will get more of it. Be warned!

One of the UK's big parcel carriers was having far too many complaints and great problems with its public image through parcels not arriving on time and at the wrong places.

Many of the parcels were being returned to the depots as undelivered due to drivers' claims that people were not in or they couldn't find the right address. So the company launched an incentive programme for the drivers based upon the fewer parcels returned to the depot, the more the drivers were rewarded in their incentive programme. Now you can imagine the result. The returns dropped dramatically but the delivery rate did not increase as parcels disappeared over hedges and on to other people's doorsteps!

Pocket Reminders

The five Golden Rules for successful incentive contests are:

▓ Everyone must have a chance to win
▓ Time the incentive system carefully
▓ Decide *exactly* what the scheme should achieve
▓ Give tangible prizes
▓ Ensure the scheme is fully understood

Wise Words

It is more important to do the right things than to do things right.

Peter Drucker

12

Motivational Communication

People are said to judge leaders more by what they do than by what they say. But it is actually what leaders express either through verbal or written communication that will make the difference to how they will be judged.

Perhaps the most major cause of strife and problems throughout the world is breakdown in communications. This can often be as simple as a misunderstanding.

The American Management Association is quoted as stating: 'A supervisor's number one challenge today can be summed up in one word – COMMUNICATIONS.'

Unfortunately, many supervisors and managers don't believe that it is necessary to keep people informed. They operate with the attitude that people have jobs to do and ought to get on and do them – and not waste time talking.

This is a very short-sighted view. Management activity in any organization cannot take place without full and open two-way communications. That means speaking as well as listening.

This can go too far, however, and people can spend *too much* time talking to each other, making their work time less productive. When people in a company are speaking to each other they are not earning the company revenue. Of course, this is necessary, and I am not saying that people should not communicate with each other, but it is essential for you and your employees to understand we only earn revenue when we are talking to potential customers and existing customers. I even see the ridiculous abuse of probably the world's greatest communication tool, e-mail, where people sitting back to back to each other will be exchanging e-mails.

One particular client company of mine, a major in the FMCG (fast-moving consumer goods) industry, was, I discovered, so riddled with internal politics that all the executives were performing for each other instead of for their customers. If the same levels of performance and customer care were channelled in the direction of their customers, they would certainly have had an even more successful business.

The first and possibly the most important rule of communication is to make clear the message being communicated. Communication will never have the desired effect if the other person doesn't comprehend the meaning. No manager can get the desired results through an incomplete or misunderstood message.

In this chapter we will be looking at communication through the written word, on the telephone and, of course, face to face. One of the big advantages of face-to-face communication is that you are in the best position to see if the person to whom you are communicating has understood the message – either through what they say or the information communicated by their body language.

A successful motivated manager understand and reads people's body language. I understand that less than 10 per cent of all communication skills are verbal. So the real art of communication is the ability to convey information or a message from one person to another with absolute clarity.

The former Home Secretary David Blunkett previously worked as leader of Sheffield Metropolitan Council, and at the time he was interviewed on the radio. The interviewer asked him whether he believed his blindness was a major disadvantage – not only in the House of Commons but also in any meetings that he had to attend. David Blunkett replied by saying that it was most certainly not a disadvantage, and to a certain extent he believed it was an advantage as, by purely listening to what people were saying, he really had to listen.

He felt he was more analytical, less emotional and less distracted by a person's body language because he was concentrating so much on the voice and the inflections.

Communication is a two-way process, giving the communicator the opportunity to respond to messages as well as give them. Any manager who can't or won't communicate well will simply never be able to do a good job or get good results.

This book is about **motivation**, so I do not intend to go into the details of how to give clear instructions. I will, however, expound more on the principles and philosophy of a motivated style of communication.

The Telephone

Let's begin with perhaps the most widely used tool of communication – the telephone. How do you and I speak to our friends, our colleagues and our employees over the phone? Take first of all the incoming phone call. When you answer the phone, sound positive and enthusiastic. When they announce their name, sound even more pleased that they are phoning you. In other words, make them feel good, make them feel important.

'How nice to hear you.'
'I am so glad you phoned.'
'It's great to hear from you.'

But always say it with a smile – it's amazing how these words sound more genuine and seem to come out more effectively when uttered by lips shaped to a smile!

Now consider the phone calls that you have to make. Plan and decide exactly what you would like to say. Again, sound positive, sound enthusiastic. If you are a manager communicating with your people, your words are extremely important. So having commenced with the courtesy or the pleasantry, 'How are you?', switch straight into the purpose of your call.

A successful sales manager, having made a brief courteous enquiry, will then ask after his or her salesperson's performance. But don't do what some managers do, namely talk about almost everything else rather than get to the point of the call. They enquire first about such mundane topics as what is in the news. **Get to the point. What is important to you also becomes important to your people.**

Many supervisors and managers use e-mail as a major tool of communication and may only meet face-to-face perhaps at a weekly or monthly meeting. The telephone becomes secondary. In such cases the telephone communication takes on an even greater importance. It becomes an opportunity to re-motivate and re-enthuse. The manager should always plan on having some good news to pass on down the line. Managers must urgently take on board this very important concept – e-mail is not a management tool and is only of real value for the exchange of important information. To communicate more effectively, don't use e-mail; use the telephone.

The manager should keep staff well informed of news, developments and all changes and opportunities. Remember the expression, 'Let them hear it from the horse's mouth.' Also, if I can refer back to my previous chapter, remember to talk about promotions or contests that may be in operation.

While on the subject of the telephone, always try to take your incoming calls: you should never be too busy. Avoid being endlessly tied up in meetings. Also, if you are absent from the office, make sure that useless information is not being passed out.

I remember phoning one manager at 12.45 pm and being told that he was out to lunch. I enquired: 'When will he be back?', and was told 'Around 3.15'. All I needed to be told was that my contact was out of the office and would be returning at about 3.15 pm.

At the end of every telephone call, see if you can leave the other person thinking 'I am glad I spoke to you today.' The telephone is an opportunity to motivate and inspire, so use it well!

Face-to-face Meetings

How do people arrive at the office first thing in the morning? How do managers and supervisors greet their employees? And while I am asking these questions, let me ask you what sort of people you want to have working with you? Positive, enthusiastic, dedicated, 'raring to go' types? Of course you do. In which case, change must start with you.

These first greetings in the morning are so important. And just as important as what we say is our appearance and body language.

Enthusiasm is infectious, so always have a positive message. Become a carrier of good news. Be consistent and not moody. People are much more secure under a management style that is consistent. And, above everything else, keep problems away from those who they do not concern. Now I am not saying that you shouldn't keep people informed – of course you should. Managers and leaders, apart from the recognition they get, normally earn more, and for this they have a greater responsibility. Within this greater responsibility they have problems that require solving, solutions that they have to find. Only weak managers will dump their worries and problems on their teams. Don't get your people worrying about your worries. It is more than likely that they cannot help, and they should not be asked to solve your problems anyhow.

Rumour-mongering causes strife

In most organizations strife is often caused through rumours.

Try to recall the last rumour that did the rounds in your organization. Just how true or how distorted was it? How destructive was it?

Most rumours appear to be fairly harmless, but they can reduce morale and damage productivity. Now, we can't alter human nature or prevent people from inventing rumours, listening to them, embellishing them or passing them on. But what we can all do is prevent the conditions that invite rumours.

Surely the condition that encourages rumours more than any other is secrecy, as it only makes people wonder, imagine and gossip. The more somebody tries to keep a secret, the more interesting it must be. Therefore, the more news you can give people, the less tendency they will have to invent their own.

We all need to know what is going on in the organization of which we are part. People are never going to stop thinking and talking about things that affect them – their jobs and their livelihood – and the less factual information there is, the greater the spread of misinformation will be. So before you decide to keep something really secret, think first: 'Is it really necessary?'

Good managers avoid secrecy about their jobs and work practices. They pass on all the information that they can. They make themselves available to answer questions and discuss issues with their people. I recall talking to a bank clerk some time ago and she was telling me how much she respected her boss. Her words were: 'He actually listens to me.'

It is, of course, one of the burdens of managing others that we have to listen to their problems. But let me remind you: THE PROBLEM SHARED IS THE PROBLEM HALVED.

I must mention the style of management that is known as 'pigeon management'. This is the manager who flies in, flaps around, drops a load of 'you know what' and flies off again. **Pigeon management must be avoided.**

Before leaving the subject of face-to-face communication, I must mention meetings. My feeling is that, the fewer one has, the better. The ideal number of people to have in attendance is one (in exceptional circumstances it can be two). If one has to have a lot of people, how about taking all the chairs out of the room. It is amazing how quickly people get to the point they wish to make when not sitting down.

I was given the following notice recently. It makes the point so well.

Are You Lonely?
Work On Your Own?
Hate Having To Make Decisions?
Rather Talk About It Than Do It?

HOLD A MEETING

You can get to see other people,
sleep in peace, offload decisions,
learn to write volumes of meaningless rhetoric,
feel important and impress (or bore) your colleagues.

AND ALL IN WORK TIME.

MEETINGS
The Practical
Alternative To Work

Communication

Let's now change our thinking for a minute to how people communicate with each other.

Communication, like so much of what we have discussed so far, does not just relate to the business environment but also to the social, sporting and leisure worlds. What do people say when they meet each other? Are they positive or are they negative? Are they finding fault and bitching about their managers and organization or are they communicating in a positive style?

From a business point of view, a negative group of people can become an unproductive group of people and this negativity can often start with just one person. It's the proverbial 'barrel of apples' example. It takes one bad apple to pollute the rest. And so it is with people. It takes one person with a stinking attitude to pollute and destroy the rest.

You can be absolutely sure that a negative team is not a motivated team.

It is therefore essential for all managers and leaders not only to understand the power of the negative, but also to train and educate their people on the power and the horrors of a negative attitude. Make no mistake about this – if, as a manager, you can't instil the importance of a positive atmosphere, you will never be able to achieve the results hoped for.

Written communication

I have already stated that breakdown of communication is the major cause of most of the world's strife. But there is one segment within this vast subject area that carries a significant amount of responsibility for the misery caused. This is *written* communication.

It is the most dangerous form of communication. Whenever words go on to paper in the form of letters, memos, faxes or e-mails – watch out.

More strikes and industrial problems within companies have been caused by the written word than by any other single factor. The written word in most cases will be read negatively. It is open for people to interpret in their own way the emphasis on certain words. More can be read into a written letter than is ever actually intended.

So my plea to all motivators is **never write anything other than a positive congratulatory communication**. Or if it is for the purpose of exchanging information, make sure it is very factual and specific.

If you get a letter from a superior that is critical about something you have been doing, are you motivated or demotivated?

We all know the answer! Whether the criticism was justified or not has little to do with it. **You will be demotivated.** Surely this is not the purpose of the letter.

Let me give you a true example.

A salesman received a letter from his sales manager just prior to leaving for another day's sales activity. Now this salesman was a highly motivated individual and he was trained not to foul up his attitude by worrying about the bills that might arrive in the post, so he would leave these unopened until the end of the day. But here was a letter from his boss and he opened it. It was critical of his work.

He was, of course, upset by it. He then went out on his first call, didn't make a sale (obviously), so went into a coffee shop, where he worked out his first draft reply. He proceeded to his next call, where he was also unsuccessful (obviously) and then took an extended lunchbreak to work on his second draft reply.

He then decided he really ought to contact his boss, so he cancelled his next appointment. He went to phone his boss and was told that he had gone away on a business trip for two days. The salesman did nothing for two days until his boss returned.

This was not the reaction that the sales manager was hoping for when he wrote that letter.

So if you have to write a letter to any of your people, make sure that it is good news. If you have bad news or you need to criticize somebody, tell them face-to-face, or at least over the phone so they have a chance to respond. The matter can be discussed, dealt with and cleared up.

You can then by all means say: 'I will drop you a line on the points we have discussed so that at least we both have a record and there is no misunderstanding.'

Now I do accept that if you have to fire somebody, you are legally obliged to give them a written warning. But this is not what I'm talking about here.

Watch your memos and e-mails

Internal memos and e-mails can also be very destructive. Some managers resort to memos or e-mails rather than to more direct communication. Apart from taking up time, a critical memo or e-mail sent to another person can cause even greater stress, as the recipient will wonder who else has seen the memo or been 'bcc'ed into the e-mail.

Any manager who uses only written communication should not be in a position of supervising or managing others. The best use of the written word is the clear exchange of information.

Be clear when you inform

A plumber once wrote to his Standards Authority to let it know that he found hydrochloric acid was excellent for cleaning out clogged drain pipes. The authority thanked him for his letter but added: 'The efficacy of hydrochloric acid is indisputable, but the corrosive residue is incompatible with metallic permanence.'

The plumber wrote back and said he was delighted that they had found his idea helpful!

He received this as a reply: 'Don't use hydrochloric acid – it eats hell out of the pipes.'

My final story in this chapter is taken from the military world, and is a great example of a verbal communication breakdown.

A Colonel issued the following directive to his Adjutant:

Tomorrow evening at approximately 20.00 hours, Halley's Comet will be visible in this area, an event that occurs only once every 75 years. Have the men fall out in the battalion area in fatigues, and I will explain this rare phenomenon to them. In the case of rain, we will not be able to see anything, so assemble the men in the theatre and I will show them films of it.

Adjutant to Company Commander:

By order of the Colonel, tomorrow at 20.00 hours, Halley's Comet will appear above the battalion area. If it rains, fall the men out in fatigues, then march to the theatre where this rare phenomenon will take place, something which occurs only once every 75 years.

Company Commander to Platoon Commander:

By order of the Colonel in Fatigues at 20.00 hours tomorrow evening, the phenomenal Halley's Comet will appear in the theatre. In case of rain, in the battalion area, the Colonel will give another order, something which occurs once very 75 years.

Platoon Commander to Platoon Sergeant:

Tomorrow at 20.00 hours, the Colonel will appear in the theatre with Halley's Comet, something which happens every 75 years. If it rains, the Colonel will order the comet into the battalion area.

Platoon Sergeant to the Platoon:

When it rains tomorrow at 20.00 hours, the phenomenal 75-year-old General Halley, accompanied by the Colonel, will drive his comet through the battalion area in fatigues.

Pocket Reminders

- Don't be a 'pigeon manager'
- Motivate down the telephone line
- Plan some good news
- Cut down on meetings
- Prevent rumours by not being too secretive
- Teach the power of the negative
- Always write positively

Wise Words

If they gave a reward for finding fault, some people would get rich quick.

13

Motivational Criticism

People who have a responsibility to supervise have a great number of things they have to control. Not the least of these is their own personal feelings towards their subordinates.

Managers and supervisors are, of course, human, and they do have their own likes and dislikes just like everyone else. An effective and motivated manager will, however, make sure that their feelings about their subordinates do not show. It is quite obvious that performance will suffer if an employee should feel that their immediate boss doesn't like them, treats them unjustly or favours somebody else.

From time to time it is necessary to get a person back on the rails or criticize them in order to get the performance and the results that you deserve.

Perhaps the most unpleasant of all the jobs that a manager ever has to do is to fire a person. I personally know of some managers who have become extremely ill through the sheer worry and pressure of having to make others redundant.

But in order to develop people, it is occasionally necessary for a manager to criticize an employee.

Charles Schwab, one of the most successful industrialists in American history, was quoted as saying: 'I have yet to find a man who did not do better work or put forth greater effort under a spirit of approval than under the spirit of criticism.'

We have already talked about the tremendous growth and advances in human behaviour that can be achieved with praise, approval and recognition. Now let's see how you can also achieve growth and acceptable performance through **motivational criticism.**

Why Criticize?

Let's begin by addressing the very simple question of why a manager should criticize an employee.

It should not be related to a personal like or dislike. It should primarily be because of a feeling of concern. Also, it is a manager's duty to guide his employees not only towards performance that keeps them in their job, but performance that helps them to achieve their goals – and, of course, maintains the team spirit.

The purpose of the criticism is not and should never be to destroy, but to build. In order to achieve this, ask yourself these questions, 'What exactly do I want to put right?' and 'What exactly is the desired reaction at the end of the meeting or interview?' In other words, 'What is my goal, my purpose or end result?'

The points that the manager should discuss must be constructive and not destructive. I make this point because so much criticism is not only unconstructive but is positively *destructive*. It takes very little brains to find fault. It takes a lot more brains to find a better way of doing something.

It's all very well if the manager knows what he wants to communicate, but he is communicating with another person, and that person also has the wonderful asset of the human brain. Therefore, in order to get the message across, you have to make sure that you haven't got a closed mind when communicating. At the commencement of the meeting, you must open up the other person's mind so that it becomes receptive to you. The person must be able to listen, take in, discuss and then react to the message that you are giving.

In many cases, a manager is forced into criticizing an employee because of actions that have been immensely irritating. Sometimes an employee acts irresponsibly and – even worse – with the intention of breaking some rule or acceptable work practice.

Some managers lose their temper and react immediately. In a state of fury, they criticize the subordinate. Don't do it – it does occasionally work, but it invariably destroys relationships, and will cause a dramatic loss of respect.

I came across the managing director of a construction company making these very silly communication errors. He also suffered from 'pigeon management', lacked moral courage and successfully destroyed the confidence of his supervisors and foreman to the point that they were unable to make any decisions. This, as you can imagine, compounded a difficult situation.

Other managers, perhaps out of frustration or lack of guts, have great difficulty in talking to the individual who is causing the problems, so they end up instead telling almost everybody else. This, of course, is an unfair management style.

Successful Motivational Criticism

Let's now run through the nine stages of successful motivational criticism:

Stage 1

Pick your time carefully. It can be very upsetting for a person to be criticized, maybe even over a minor mistake, when they are just about to tackle an important job.

Let me ask you this question: is it right to criticize someone on a Friday evening – just before they are going home for the weekend – when they will have little chance of putting right the points you have raised?

Stage 2

Your discussion must be in complete privacy. You know the rule – praise in public, chastise in private.

Under no circumstances whatsoever should anybody, either colleague, subordinate or superior, be able to overhear or oversee your discussion. This is common sense, but it is a mistake that so many managers make, and then they wonder why they get a hostile reaction.

In most cases, this hostility is caused by the person who is being criticized not really listening but worrying about what their colleagues will be thinking. This causes them to put up a fight, again for the benefit of the listeners. It is like playing to the gallery.

So the golden rule is – chastise in total privacy.

Stage 3

Before you mention the constructive points of criticism, make the person receptive to you; this is very simply done by letting the other person know that you do appreciate them and by listing all the good things that they do.

This can be complimentary and, as we have already discussed in previous chapters, the good manager looks to catch people doing things *right*. So this first stage, to a certain extent, is motivational, but it makes the person prepared and open minded enough to listen and discuss the problems in a reasonable fashion. Tell them their good points, remind them of their successes and achievements. Everybody has some.

Stage 4

Look the person in the eyes. The manager who is unable to look the other person in the face loses credibility and the strength of the message suffers. Some people look out of the window or at their feet and consequently they weaken dramatically what they have to say.

Stage 5

Be strictly truthful. This is not to imply that managers tend to tell lies. But what does often happen is that they have difficulty in 'telling it the way it is'. They believe that their subordinate has sufficient imagination to interpret a vague message. They rely too much on innuendo, hoping that the other person gets the point without actually saying what the point is.

So tell it the way it is. Be specific. And if it does relate to a personal characteristic – for example, where the person's appearance is letting them down – a caring manager will point this out.

We've all heard the expression that it is only a real friend who will tell you the truth; so it should be with a good, caring and motivated manager.

I remember eating a cream cake on a train and then, taking a taxi, I went into a business meeting. It was only on leaving the meeting and going into a washroom that I noticed a lump of cream on my chin. If only somebody had told me!

Stage 6

Try not to criticize a person, but do criticize the person's actions. One must be very careful not to criticize a person in what one can describe as the area of 'values and beliefs'.

There are occasions when, by criticizing behaviour, one has

to mention the cause, as we discussed in the previous stage. But this is the crux of the communication process: *behaviour* leads to the results that one wants to change or improve, and it is in this area that one must be absolutely specific and clear.

Stage 7

Having discussed the various points that are targets of criticism, the manager must then build that person up again. This is easily and effectively done by reaffirming their good points. Again, spell these out.

Let's remember the purpose of criticism. You want to send the individual out of the meeting having listened to and accepted the criticism, but also saying to themselves, 'I am going to put right what was wrong', and with the respect and loyalty between the two parties still intact.

> The purpose of criticism is not to destroy the confidence, self-image and self-belief of the other person. It is to build on in the future.

Everybody does some things right, everybody has good qualities and it is these that should be restated.

Stage 8

Now set a date with the person you have just criticized on which a review of the points discussed can take place. At some stage it may also be necessary to put a summary of the points raised into a letter so that both individuals have a record and there can be no misunderstanding. The date of the review is important, as it shows the commitment of the manager to follow through his criticism, as well as giving a goal for the subordinate to aim towards.

Stage 9

The final stage is, of course, the praise that the manager should give when the criticized person gets it right.

And we come back to that great management principle – **whatever you reward, you get more of.**

That praise is a prize in the reward stakes.

I personally find that, whenever it is necessary to criticize constructively, it is important to stress that what I am saying is my own opinion – I may be right or I may be wrong.

The Problems of Dismissal

Just before we leave the subject of criticism, the motivated manager will unfortunately, from time to time, have to dismiss an employee.

Once that decision has been taken, it should not be delayed. In most cases, to preserve the team the departure should happen as speedily as possible. There are, of course, exceptions to this rule in which people can work out a period of notice. In most cases, this is extremely dangerous and will be demotivational to the remainder of the team. It is therefore better for everybody concerned that, when that decision has been taken, the person concerned leaves the company immediately.

Any manager obviously hates having to tell an employee that their services are no longer required. Nevertheless, it is one of the burdens and responsibilities for which managers are duly rewarded.

When firing another individual, the manager should never destroy them. A manager should never set out to break down their self-image, confidence or self-belief. If the decision to dismiss has been taken, it is right to give justifiable, fair and logical reasons, so you have to communicate the truth. In some cases, however, you do not have to tell the whole truth.

If the individual does get angry or uptight, it really doesn't matter to the manager. Treat it as a 'So what?' exercise. Far better that that person goes out feeling angry, but with their attitude, beliefs and confidence intact so that they can go on to get another job, than be too demotivated even to go after one.

> Sir John Harvey-Jones, widely acclaimed as one of the great management gurus in the UK, states: 'You sometimes have to fire people. The most important thing is that you are not entitled to damage their self-esteem. It is quite difficult to avoid doing that but you have to bear in mind you are not entitled to wreck a man's life for your business purpose.'

One of the things I tend to say is: 'Look, I am extremely sorry. You are an able person but the chemistry just doesn't work – you'll have to blame me.'

I would much rather take the responsibility of being disliked than the responsibility of looking at someone and thinking that I wrecked that person's life.

Pocket Reminders

To criticize *without* demotivating, you must:

- ▨ Pick your time carefully
- ▨ Discuss the matter in private
- ▨ Let the person know you value them
- ▨ Look them in the eyes
- ▨ Be strictly truthful
- ▨ Criticize behaviour, not the person
- ▨ Reaffirm the person's good points
- ▨ Set a review date

And remember to praise improvement!

Wise Words

Insincere praise is worse than no praise at all.

14

Success Through People

As I have already stated many times, success is only achieved through people. This means that a manager or supervisor gets results not just from their own efforts – far greater results are achieved by duplication and from moulding people into a cohesive team.

We have discussed leadership and communication and we have looked at the principles of effective leadership styles, as well as the importance of motivational communication.

In this chapter I want firstly to look at giving instructions that get results and then secondly at effective delegation.

Giving Instructions

Every supervisor and manager has to give other people instructions and orders from time to time. It is sometimes the case that these instructions are given at conferences or seminars, where senior managers have to lay out new strategy, methods of operation and in many cases changes of policy or even work practice. In my book *Communicate to Win*, the techniques to use for these occasions are covered in great detail, so I will not attempt to duplicate that information here. I will concentrate instead on the thinking behind developing the willingness, the enthusiasm and, of course, the motivation to grasp the messages being communicated and to put them into practice. This is just as important as giving the instructions or orders themselves.

I was once the guest speaker at one of the UK's major insurance company's seminars. They had all the senior executives gathered and were launching the company's new strategy that had taken some two and a half years of very expensive research and development to devise. The detail that unfolded was the most impressive that I have ever experienced.

Every single piece of the new plan had been diligently thought through before the launch date and presentation – apart from the people factor. They had prepared the systems, the paperwork and the organizational structure, but they had completely neglected the reactions of the workforce. The tremendous fear and the lack of confidence that the word 'change' provokes and the necessary personal development needed to make the programme a success had been overlooked. In short, the motivation required for the employees to implement the new strategy successfully was totally lacking and the reaction was negative, not positive. If only the managers had realized the importance of **personal development training.**

My second example is a major name in the food and drinks industry. This company also decided that it was time for a change to its operational structure, from a vertical line of communication to a more lateral approach.

The new strategy was launched to the senior executives. Some three months later the whole exercise had to be repeated to exactly the same group. It was rapidly discovered that the messages and changes that had been communicated were not being taken on board, nor were they in any way operational.

In this instance, the strategy the first time around had been unclearly communicated and also, just as in my first example, motivation was totally lacking. The executives left the first event without that deep-seated drive to put the changes into practice.

People must be inspired, motivated and sold new ideas, strategy or methods for improved performance. So much of my work involves speaking at conferences, conventions and seminars with the purpose of helping people to feel the confidence, the belief in themselves and the motivation to get up and go.

Instructions and orders do not necessarily always revolve around a change of work practice. But, in any circumstances, the manager should be using verbal communication to impart tasks or responsibility that lead towards the organization's collective goal.

Motivational Communication

Let's run through six ideas for giving instructions and orders that *do* get results, that *do* build the 'want' and that form a motivational style of management communication. Let me once again state emphatically that the process is verbal and not written, although it can be followed up in some written form afterwards.

1. Make it clear what the order or instruction is. Common sense, I know – but far too many people in authority do not spell out exactly what is required in its simplest form. They often understand the situation so well themselves that they assume the other person knows what they are talking about.

2. How about getting people to repeat your instructions in their own words? Many people, on being given an instruction, will not admit that they do not fully understand all of what is being said or is expected of them, particularly if they feel their manager is impatient.

3. Encourage people to discuss and ask questions. Don't give the impression that you would be irritated or annoyed if a question were asked.

   By allowing people to ask questions, you increase their involvement and participation. This also reduces the risk of misunderstanding and develops opportunities for clarification. 'How do you feel about... ?' 'What do you think?' 'Have you any ideas?'

4. Try *asking* rather than telling. The motivational manager knows he gets greater success through people by asking pleasantly rather than barking out an order.

   The 'Can you please despatch that package today?' rather than 'I want that package despatched today' or, even worse, 'Despatch that package today'.

   'Will you please get that report completed by lunchtime?' is better than 'Get that report completed by lunchtime.'

   The way you ask people to do things makes such a difference, both to the relationship that develops between you and to the cooperation you will get. By asking, you will also avoid resentment.

5. Do tell the individual *why*. This can just be a brief explanation; when somebody understands why a certain instruction needs to be carried out, it not only makes their job more interesting, but will help them to understand your point of view more effectively. A person who understands why they are carrying out a task is far less likely to make a mistake.

   They will also become more committed and involved, and if the job becomes unnecessary, they will have enough sense not to continue. On the other hand, if they don't understand the reason for doing the job, they will blindly go on doing what they have been told to do.

6. Do follow up. Staying in touch is one of the most successful methods of preventing little problems from becoming much larger ones. It also has the added advantage that people will look forward to giving you information on their progress and it will encourage successful and positive results from them.

   People hate imparting bad news to their manager, so if they know that they are going to be asked to discuss something, their commitment and determination to succeed will be so much stronger.

   Careful handling is needed in certain situations.

Some people lack confidence, others are very sensitive or, at the other extreme, have an ego problem. Such people may have to be coached into believing that the idea or reason for the instruction was theirs.

The conversation can go something like, 'How do you feel this should be handled?', and after their response, the reply can be, 'I thought you were going to say that' or 'I thought that was what you were really thinking.'

The six most important words are: 'I admit I made a mistake'.
The five most important words are: 'I am proud of you'.
The four most important words are: 'What is your opinion?'
The three most important words are: 'If you please'.
The two most important words are: 'Thank you'.
The most important word is: 'We'.
The least important word is: 'I'.

Delegation

Success comes through people. The great leaders and managers of the world surely have at least two things in common. Firstly, they have a desire to employ people with greater skills or knowledge than they themselves possess, and secondly, they have an ability to develop people into leaders. In other words, they look for ways to duplicate themselves in other people.

Developing people is achieved by careful and planned delegation of responsibility and duty. No manager will ever achieve very much if they try to carry the whole burden of management on their shoulders.

There are four stages to successful delegation:

1. Assume that people who work for you have ability. Managers must make that assumption. They must have that confidence and belief in their subordinates. By showing that they have that confidence in their staff, most people will rise to the level of ability that their manager is assuming they have.

We have said earlier: 'It is not ability but desire that creates success.' Abilities can be learned, and if a manager shows their own confidence in an individual's abilities, this will in turn increase the person's desire if the ability is at present limited.

2. When delegating a job, leave as little doubt as possible in the employee's mind as to what is expected. Tell the individual:

   (a) what should be done;
   (b) why it is needed;
   (c) when it should be completed.

3. *But do not tell them how.* This is the secret of successful delegation. When you tell somebody exactly how you want a task carried out, it removes any creativity. It becomes completely boring, there is no challenge and they do not have to develop in any capacity whatsoever. But by not telling them how, it does create a challenge. It gets the brain working. It will no doubt create some stress or excitement, but it gives the individual a chance to think.

   You might say 'My tasks are far too important to risk a mistake', in which case you can ask the person to work out the best way of tackling the task, but to check with you before actually proceeding. This, of course, does give you a safety net and perhaps fewer sleepless nights!

4. Finally, the motivational manager will, of course, always give credit and praise generously if a person does a good job.

   If, on the other hand, they do a lousy job (which is unlikely if you have followed the above stages), whatever you do, don't make a great deal of it. They will know they have done a lousy job. They will also have a lack of confidence, and if you are a motivational leader, they will almost certainly not make that mistake again. But the experience will have been an educational one through which they will be a greater asset and a better employee in the future.

Pocket Reminders

The four stages of successful delegation are:

■ Assume sufficient ability
↓
■ Explain the task, but
↓
■ Do not detail exactly *how* the job must be done
↓
■ Credit where credit is due

Wise Words

No person who does not feel genuine joy in the success of those under them or those that have been under them will ever be a great leader.

Richard Denny

15

Motivation at Home

The world in which we all live and work is purely a people's world.

Throughout this book I have been concentrating on the ideals of people-to-people motivational communication – as well as the principles of self-motivation – with the common objective of achieving greater success and happiness.

As people climb the career ladder, they are expected to give greater commitment, loyalty and work hours to their employer. For many, work becomes all-absorbing and, tragically, they get the proportion of time and effort spent on living and working out of balance. The work/life balance is now taking on, and rightly so, a new importance

The purpose of living becomes the work: they become so involved that eventually they become workaholics. They become so dedicated and committed to the company and to their business responsibilities that they wreak havoc and destruction upon their own home environment. For those who are self-employed, their business and their involvement in it becomes all-encompassing, taking over the whole of their lives.

Surely the purpose of work is that it is a means to an end? It is not the end itself. Surely we work to provide money, which in turn sustains a lifestyle that provides the pleasure or happiness that we all seek?

The joys of life seem only to be important when shared with others. Happiness and pleasure really only come from other people. Yet many executives and high-flyers in the business world unwittingly destroy what they set out to achieve.

We are all too well aware of the high rate of divorce in western society. There are, of course, countless reasons as to why there is a greater chance of marriage breakup in this decade than 30 or 50 years ago. It is partly due to the decreased stigma attached to divorce, the relative ease of getting a divorce, and also to the pressures and temptations of 21st-century living.

But there is unlikely to be any let-up in the demands on people to achieve success, either through their own business efforts or through the companies by which they are employed.

I have discussed this point with many executives and it is very sad how many are deeply shocked and surprised when their own marriage goes wrong. They initially blame their partner, but this bitterness turns into remorse and terrible self-blame.

They talk about how hard they worked, the evenings and weekends they gave purely to their company, the dedication and commitment they gave in order to achieve promotion and higher salaries. And all this for the sole purpose of providing a bigger or better house, greater luxuries for their home, education for their children and financial security for their partners. They did it for their partner, yet they fail to understand that happiness and pleasure does not come from money but from sharing.

You must have the power of empathy to put yourself in your partner's shoes.

Health and Well-being

Doctors' surgeries up and down the country are filled with

patients who are not ill, but lonely or depressed. These are people who have no hope, nothing to look forward to, nobody with whom to share their own innermost thoughts and feelings, who feel unloved or uncared for.

They suffer from illnesses of the mind as opposed to bodily diseases, ailments or complaints, which follow on rapidly from an unhappy mental outlook.

People who are happy, who are motivated and who are striving for success are much less likely to ever visit a doctor's surgery. Statistics show that people who are self-employed are far less likely to be ill or to visit their doctor than those who are employed by someone else. Why? One could draw the simple conclusion that those who are self-employed can't afford to be ill and there has to be an element of truth in that.

But again, as with all these points, there are the exceptions to the rule. A person who is continually striving for success and works evenings and weekends is under enormous pressure and could be more likely to suffer from heart disease than another person who takes life more easily.

Workaholics

Some people will justify their workaholic approach as being for the benefit of their family. But in many cases it is for their own self-gratification that they are striving. Then they find all too late the misery, the loneliness and the desperation of having nobody with whom to share that success or achievement.

Motivation is really about people. It is concerned with achieving success for the individual as well as for the group, team or organization. Lasting or progressive success can only be maintained while the foundation of purpose remains intact: the human gratification that comes from sharing.

Any person therefore who can convince themself that they are a great motivator at work, when they are not loved, respected or cherished at home, must be a fraud.

The person who adheres to the principles in this book in

their working life will be successful. But those who ignore the same principles in their home environment will create havoc and misery. And in the end this will destroy their ability to inspire or motivate others. It's the 'practise what I preach' syndrome. Ask yourself – DO YOU?

Balancing Work and Play

Life is all about balance and maintaining the equilibrium. Too much of one thing in either direction and you've got it wrong. So now let's run through a few thoughts and ideas that can help to maintain the balance and the purpose of life.

Every person who is in the fortunate position of sharing their life with another (and that can be their children, their partners or other members of their family) experiences the 'thrill' of the sound of the person's footsteps as they arrive home.

This surely has to be a prime motivator for all of us – when those who are at home are excited at the sound of us returning.

This can be so easily achieved by, firstly, caring and, secondly, planning. As we have said continually, people spend so much time planning their work, why don't they also plan their home activities?

I do accept that people plan their holidays, but this may be for only two or three weeks per year. What about the other 50-odd weeks?

Plan events at home. They can be a visit to a friend, a drive in the country, the theatre, the cinema or a meal out. The list of things to do is endless. Invite friends to visit, but above everything else find opportunities for the family to share hobbies and interests. There is a wonderful expression that says: 'A family that plays together, stays together.'

In creating a motivated home life it is essential for partners to discuss their goals. They must collectively decide what these are and both parties must be actively involved in pursuing the goals.

The partner who has been away at work should recognize

what has been going on at home. This may sound superficial but take it in the way it's meant. Recognize the new hairstyle. Recognize the meals that are served. Recognize the work that goes on in any average home.

I do accept that in many households nowadays, two people go out to work, but not in every household and I personally love the description of the one who stays at home as being the 'Home Executive'. Where both go out to work home responsibilities should, of course, be shared. And you could play the game where the first person home thinks up a nice surprise to greet the other when he or she gets back.

Spending too much time at weekends with your own personal hobbies or interests should be avoided. It can be terribly selfish when a partner spends the greater proportion of their free time purely involved in their own hobby or interest.

Communication at home is just as important as it is at work. Try creating opportunities for all members of the family to talk. It is important that families should all sit down for a meal together and chat. By talking more and on a regular basis there is less chance of conflict or strife within a family unit.

For people who are fortunate enough to become parents, it is essential that they do not miss the events in their children's upbringing: school plays, sports days and speech days should take priority over any business activity. How often have we heard parents say that their children grew up so fast that they missed sharing their pleasures and successes with them?

And finally, the greatest gift a parent can give to his or her children is an understanding of the power and the damaging effects of negative thinking and the power and potential of positive thinking – the 'You can' rather than the 'You can't'.

The person who practises and believes in true motivation at home will be a more successful motivator at work.

Finally

Take yourself in hand. Have you got it right? What are your

priorities? There is a trend where people are expected to work longer and longer hours. What is important is not the hours spent at work, but what you achieve in those hours. I cannot believe that anybody's final thoughts as they depart from this world are 'I wish I had spent more time at work'. It is not difficult for people in management to take a three-day weekend perhaps twice a month. It is highly motivational for yourself and for those that you share your life with. We are conditioned to strive for achievement, and achievement is not just work related or money in the bank.

Pocket Reminders

■ Motivation does not stop when you get home
■ Plan collective goals
■ Recognize achievement
■ Avoid becoming egocentric
■ Communicate more and often
■ Remember that priorities should include elements of your home life

---

Wise Words

Fear less, hope more; eat less, chew more;
Whine less, breathe more; talk less, say more;
Hate less, love more;
And all good things are yours.

Swedish proverb

Summary

This book, *Motivate to Win*, as I am sure you have found by now, contains some of the great principles and philosophies of success and achievement.

Motivation, as we started off by saying, requires the foundation of hope. What is it that you want in your life? A better job? A new home? Good health? A happy marriage? Fame, fortune, success?

Whatever it is, it is available and you can have it. **You can have anything you really want, but you cannot have everything you want.** The more you think about this statement, the more acceptable and realistic your genuine goals become.

Whatever the crisis, problem or situation you may be confronted with, it is crucial to be single-minded and keep your goal in focus while deciding on the action to take. So many people make the mistake of letting either their ego or their emotions come between them and their goal. Some people try to score points, whereas others feel they have to prove or emphasize their authority.

Ask yourself these questions when faced with difficult situations:

■ 'Is this action going to take me towards my goal – yes or no?'
■ 'Is what I am saying or doing going to get the result I really want?'

Think of the consequences before taking the action. Your goals should be the purpose of every action that you take.

This book has been subtitled 'How to Motivate Yourself and Others'. For what? Hopefully, for a greater achievement to succeed – you must be willing to do whatever it takes to win. Please understand that winning is a frame of mind and that is more important than the doing or the action. The willingness precedes the action. It is so easy to justify weakness, reject goals as unrealistic or be cynical, but you CAN have anything you really want. Be willing to do more, be willing to take whatever honourable action is required. Initially, there may well be some sacrifices, but shortly you will enjoy the rewards of achievement and success.

Perhaps one of your most intangible goals is to become and *remain* a motivated person. Yes, you can be – ALWAYS.

Refer back to this book regularly. Dip into the various check lists. Remind yourself of the principles – and remember: as a motivated person, you can't help but motivate others.

YES, YOU DO HAVE THE ABILITY WITHIN YOU!

Accept responsibility for making things the way they are and assume responsibility for changing them. Enjoy the responsibilities of being a motivator.

GOOD LUCK, GREAT SUCCESS!!!

It Can be Done

Somebody said that it couldn't be done
But he, with a chuckle, replied
That maybe it couldn't but he would be one
Who wouldn't say so 'til he tried.

So he buckled right in, with a trace of a grin
On his face, if he worried he hid it;
He started to sing as he tackled the thing
That couldn't be done, and he did it.

There are thousands to tell you it cannot be done;
There are thousands to prophesy failure;
There are thousands to point out to you one by one
The dangers that wait to assail you.

But just buckle right in with a bit of a grin
Throw off your coat and go to it;
Just start to sing as you tackle the thing
That cannot be done, and you'll do it.

Anon

Richard Denny's books are all available from good booksellers or direct from the publishers at:

Kogan Page Ltd
120 Pentonville Road
London N1 9JN
Telephone: 0207 278 0433
Facsimile: 0207 837 6348
E-mail: kpinfo@kogan-page.co.uk
Website: www.kogan-page.co.uk

For further information on Richard Denny's books, videos, audio cassettes and CDs, please write to:

The Richard Denny Group
8 Cotswold Business Village
Moreton-in-Marsh
Gloucestershire GL56 0JQ

Telephone: 00 44 + (0) 1608 651597
Facsimile: 00 44 + (0) 1608 651638
E-mail: success@denny.co.uk

Or visit the website www.denny.co.uk for your motivational message of the day.

Kogan Page is Europe's largest independent publisher of business books.

Kogan Page books cover every key business function – including management, marketing, branding, finance, sales, human resources, training, logistics, and transport – at every level from basic skills to high-level academic and professional texts. We also publish titles on careers and personal development, property, personal finance and general reference.

We have co-publishing relationships with many leading corporations, professional firms, media, institutions, professional bodies, and government and overseas agencies.